I AM FEARFULLY AND WONDERFULLY MADE

THIS IS OUR IDENTITY
(PSALMS 139:14)

By the Grace of God We Are What We Are
For in Him We Live and Move and Have Our Being
And We Can Do All Things Through Jesus Christ

ANTHONY B. POWELL

PRESS

ISBN 9781629525679

www.xulonpress.com

CONTENTS

Reality Three – By The Grace of God I Am What I Am

ACKNOWLEDGEMENTS

"For though you have ten thousand instructors in Christ, yet have you not many fathers: for in Christ Jesus I have begotten you through the gospel" (1 Corinthians 4:15).

Being spiritually minded and having a well-rounded spiritual life are essential elements in our spiritual growth and maturity. Though we have many who offer their services as our instructors, we only have one spiritual father. That one person in my life is Bishop Rodney S. Walker, with Heritage Church International and General Overseer, Bishop R S Walker Ministries. I wish to acknowledge Bishop Walker dedication and commitment to my spiritual growth and pouring out into me, developing an intimate father-son relationship and for bringing and releasing me into the Office of the Prophet. Further, under his leadership and tutelage I received the necessary training and guidance to function as a Prophetic Presbyter and assist Bishop Walker in raising prophets of characters through the Another Touch of Glory School of the Prophets.

I also want to acknowledge two other wonderful people who have had a spiritual significance in my spiritual life, growth and maturity. First, my pastor, Bishop Melvin E. Blake, JR, In His Imagine Christian Ministries. Bishop Blake's leadership, love for the people of God and his compassion and nurturing nature are truly a Godsend and blessing to the Body of Christ. I acknowledge and thank Bishop Blake for the last 15 years of his pastoral care, providing a spiritual covering while giving me occasions to preach and teach the gospel and provide me with opportunities to function in a leadership role. Second, Reverend Doctor Joseph E. Powell, JR, Covenant Lifehouse Ministries. My brother in Jesus Christ, as well as my natural brother and fondly known as "Poochie" for his ability to uniquely blend humor and wit with the word of God to impact and change lives for the glory and kingdom of God.

INTRODUCTION

As a Body of Believers, we have allowed flesh, the enemy, trials, tribulations, distresses, persecutions, famines, nakedness, perils, circumstances and situations to steal our identity. *Identity theft* occurs when someone pretends to be another by assuming that person's identity, typically in order to access resources, credit and other benefits in that person's name. Oftentimes, the identity thief attempts to block the victim's true identity while masquerading with our identity in tow. The identity thief wants to take over his victim's life, causing it to spiral out of control into a life of pain, misery, hopelessness, confusion and frustration. The identity thief comes with a single mission in mind – to steal, kill and destroy the Believer in Jesus Christ.

The identity thief not only robs Believers of their God-given identity, he also drastically affects our calling in Jesus Christ, fulfillment and families. By blocking and concealing our identity, the enemy can blind us to the power and authority of God's holy word. As a Body of Believers, we need to realize and embrace our God-given identity if we are to glorify God to the fullest and fulfill His purpose and destiny in our lives.

Our God and Father fearfully and wonderfully made us in His image and likeness so that we can have an identity and fulfill three realities – *to God be the glory, I can do what the Word says I can do and by the grace of God I am what I am*. He also gives us an identity uniquely tailored to and woven into His sacred and holy word. God's word ultimately leads one to conclude and believe God's three realities for humanity. Our flesh is probably the greatest challenge that our identity has to face and overcome, especially if we are not used to living our lives according to God's holy word and His three realities.

SUMMARY OF GOD'S THREE REALITIES FOR HUMANITY

TO GOD BE THE GLORY – REALITY ONE

To understand this first reality, we need to understand that we can do all things through Jesus Christ who strengthens us and makes us what we are to the glory of God. Glorifying God should be the barometer that drives us and the mandate that guides all our actions and deeds.

Seeing the face of God means that we have tapped into His glory. Upon doing so we can do what He does. Even though God is everywhere, He does not readily show His face and His divine favor because not every Believer has exercised the special rights and privileges required to be able to look into God's face. Only those who diligently seek the Lord and aim for His glory can have a divine face-to-face encounter with the Lord, as a man speaks unto his friend. When we have this divine face-to-face encounter with the

Lord, He allows us the privilege of gently touching and turning His face towards our face. It is in this moment that we come face-to-face with God's glory.

I CAN DO WHAT THE WORD SAYS I CAN DO – REALITY TWO

As Believers, we need to embrace the very words Jesus Christ spoke when He said that we shall not only do the works He did, but greater works than He did. Failing to do what the word says we are able to do is a major problem facing the Body of Christ today. Most Believers will quickly state that they believe what the word of God says, yet oftentimes refuse to do those things the word says they can do. Instead, they desire to walk in what our flesh is wanting and in how they feel or the "I feel good *fleshly* syndrome." As Believers, we must come to a place in God where we become "doers" of His word and realize that when we believe on Jesus Christ, we are able to do not only the works that Christ did, but even greater works. When we do what the word says we can do, we will receive whatsoever things which we say shall come to pass and nothing shall be impossible for us.

BY THE GRACE OF GOD I AM WHAT I AM – REALITY THREE

When Moses had a divine encounter with God, he asked Him, "When I come unto the children of Israel and shall say unto them, The God of your Fathers hath sent me unto you and they shall say to me, What is His name? What shall I say unto them?" God said unto Moses, "I AM THAT I AM" (Exodus 3:13-14). At this divine moment in eternity, God did not hesitate to reveal His identity to Moses and was very clear and precise about it. Just as God was with Moses, He wants Believers to be clear and precise about our identity. In 1 Corinthians 15:10 the word of God tells us that "by the grace of God I am what I am."

EMBRACING THE THREE REALITIES

Believers embracing these three realities will soon begin to walk in the word, display the power of the word and exercise the authority of the word. Eventually, the Believers will understand their iden-tity in the Father, which will propel, motivate and drive them to glorify our Father and Creator, for in Him we live and move and have our being (Acts 17:28). Furthermore, Believers will come to realize that we can do what the word says we can do, and by the grace of God we are what we are because God, our Father, fearfully and wonderfully made us so.

TO GOD BE THE GLORY

Reality One

"Now unto the King eternal, immortal, invisible, the only wise God, be honor and glory forever and ever. Amen" (1 Timothy 1:17).

To God be the glory–God fearfully and wonderfully made us so that we might have perfect fellowship and intimacy with Him, to be in His perfect will, to possess His nature, to walk in His glory and to give Him glory. We can do all things through Jesus Christ who strengthens and makes us what we are to the glory of God. Glorifying God should be the barometer that drives our actions. Further, to God be the glory should be the mandate that guides our actions and deeds. In other words, our actions and deeds should glorify the Father and we should model our behavior after Jesus Christ when He lifted His eyes to heaven and said, *"Father, the hour is come, glorify thy Son, that thy Son also may glorify thee"* (John 17:1, 4).

Chapter 1

SHOW ME THY GLORY

"And he said, I beseech thee, shew me thy glory" (Exodus 33:18).

Moses said to God, "I beseech thee, show me thy glory." Moses' deep yearning and desire to see more of God created an intense desire within to experience the fullness of God's glory. ***God's glory*** is the essence of God, Himself. Glory brings God's manifested presence, or the hand of God, near. When the fullness of God's glory manifests itself, man is forced to step aside and move with God's glory. Everything God wants to manifest is in His glory and He will not give it to anyone because that is the essence of who He is (Isaiah 42:8).

While God jealously guards His glory, He will allow us to encounter the residue or lingering presence of His glory until we become so saturated with His glory that it drips off of us. Moses, Elisha, Paul and Timothy experienced this reality firsthand. Moses' face shone with the glory of God after he was with the Lord for 40 days and 40 nights (Exodus 34:29-30, 35). Elisha also had face-to-face encounters with the glory of God to such an extent that even his buried bones remained saturated with God's glory. After his death a band of Moabites cast a dead man into the sepulcher of Elisha, and when the dead man's body touched Elisha's bones he revived and stood up on his feet (2 Kings 13:20-21).

Likewise, Paul's desire for face-to-face encounters with God and to see His glory was fulfilled by God working special miracles by the hands of Paul so that "from his body were brought unto the sick handkerchiefs or aprons and the diseases departed from them and the evil spirits went out of them" (Acts 19:11-12). Peter also experienced face-to-face encounters with the Lord which enabled God to cause Peter's shadow to drip with His glory so that the mere passing of it healed sick people (Acts 5:15). Imagine that! Moses' face shone with God's glory, Elisha's buried bones saturated with God's glory brought a dead man back to life a year after his death, Paul's handkerchiefs or aprons healed diseases and Peter's shadow cured sicknesses. What all four of these individuals had in common were their desires for God to show them

His glory, face-to-face encounters with God, God's saturated glory dripping from them and their desire to declare His glory among the nations and His wonders among all people (Psalm 96:3).

We, likewise, can experience these same face-to-face encounters with God. However, it is vitally important for us to understand that we will have to pay a price in order to come face-to-face with God's glory. The price God requires of us in order for Him to show us His glory is for us to die to self (flesh). God declared that flesh would not glory in His presence (1 Corinthians 1:29). Therefore, something dies within us every time we encounter God's glory. God says to the Body of Christ that He must increase but we must decrease in the presence of His glory (John 3:30).

When part of our flesh dies, more of our spirit lives and all that is of the Spirit lives forever in His glory. The more dying and decaying flesh God smells, the closer He can come to show His glory. God cannot come close to "living" flesh because it reeks of the world and the "stench" of man. Further, dying to our self (flesh) brings one into agreement with God's will and makes it possible to go beyond the veil.

Chapter 2

GOING BEYOND THE VEIL

*"And, behold, the veil of the temple was rent in
twain from the top to the bottom; and the earth
did quake and the rocks rent" (Matthew 27:51).*

The time has come for us to step through and enter
the Most Holy Place where God our Holy Father
resides in all His preeminence, His holiness, His righteousness, the essence of His love, His power and His
authority. Jesus Christ not only gave Believers a new
and living way, which He consecrated for us, through
the veil – His flesh, His death also caused the veil to
become torn from top to bottom. This tearing of the
veil was done to ensure that every Believer has personal access to God. Subsequently, Believers now can
boldly enter into the Holy of Holies to have a divine
face-to-face encounter with God beyond the veil
(Matthew 27:51; Hebrews 4:16; Hebrews 10:19-20).

It is extremely important for us to understand that within the veil all is Spirit. Within the veil we shall abide under the shadow of the Almighty. Within the veil, the King of Glory covers us with the essence of His being and protects us with His Spirit. When we go beyond the veil we become invisible to Satan. The reason is that when we are beyond the veil, Satan and the enemy cannot tell the difference between us and God because we appear as the image of God, act like God and sound like God. Within the veil the only thing Satan can see is all God and more of God. Beyond the veil Satan, sickness, disease and depression cannot touch us. Whatever we see within the veil we see by the light of the living and Almighty God. Within the veil is the Lord, I AM THAT I AM, Alpha and Omega, the Almighty, the King of Glory! Within the veil an inti-macy waits for us that is so deep we cannot even begin to imagine it outside of the veil. In the Most Holy Place beyond the veil we experience an utter abandonment to His will and desire for us! Beyond the veil we see things as God sees them—that all things are possible!

At this moment in eternity God is saying "come up hither, come up higher and walk with Me within the veil, come with Me in boldness beyond the veil. I have given you personal access to Me beyond the veil. Take my hand and I will lead you there where the King of Glory most certainly prevails." Beyond the veil your spirit will know with all certainty that the King of Glory is the Lord, strong and mighty and mighty in battle.

As we approach the veil, the Spirit of the living God whispers gently in our ears calling us to enter behind the veil, to leave the "I feel good *fleshly* syndrome" outside of the veil, to bow down before and embrace His Almighty presence and the essence of His being beyond the veil; to forget those things which are behind, to reach forward to those things beyond the veil and press toward the mark of the high calling of God in Jesus Christ.

As we come even closer to the veil, the Holy Spirit beckons us to come all the way in beyond the veil, to step into intimacy and rest in the depths of God's heart. We then hear a voice from heaven that sounds like the voice of many waters and as the voice of a great thunder crying out to us to come dwell with the King of Glory, to enter into the secret place of the Almighty and hide in the secret of God's presence, to go and abide with God behind the veil because in His presence is where we will most certainly prevail. The Holy Spirit and the voice from heaven are sweetly calling us. They are lovingly calling us to a place beyond the veil, to a place where God is, to a place where God lives and arises, to a place full of God's glory. All this and more than the eye has seen, the ear has heard and what has entered in the heart await us in the place God has prepared to those who dare yield to the call and go beyond the veil.

Prayer

"Father, our God, which is in Heaven cause me to hear your voice as you call me to come up higher and take a place by You on Your holy hill. Teach me how not to look at and pursue your anointing but seek a divine face-to-face encounter with You. Father, I pray that You show me Your glory. Show me Your glory is my deepest desire. I long to see Your face, show me Your glory is my desire. Prepare me now through your divine wisdom and the impartation of your Holy Spirit to accept, walk in and carry Your glory. Prepare me Lord to have a divine face-to-face encounter with You and to ascend into the hill of the Lord and stand in Your holy place. Bow down oh Lord, Bow down oh Lord as you hear my cry for a divine face-to-face encounter, show me Your glory and ready my heart to receive the King of Glory. In Jesus Christ's name I do pray, Amen"

Chapter 3

LINGERING AND DANCING IN FRONT OF THE VEIL

"That no flesh should glory in His presence"
(1 Corinthians 1:29).

T here is more of God available to us than we are ever capable of imagining. Sadly, we have become accustomed to and satisfied with merely lingering and dancing in front of the veil rather than yearning for the glory that lies within. We must learn to press beyond the veil and desire to go where God dwells. Our flesh holds us back and prevents us from going beyond the veil into the Most Holy Place where we will encounter God's face and His divine glory. Our flesh's desire is for us to dance before the veil and occasionally attempt to peek beyond it. Nevertheless, despite all the vain attempts to catch a glimpse of what is on the other side, our flesh decides it is better to stay outside of the veil. This why we must be like John the Baptist who said he must decrease and die to self (flesh). We have to remember that having a greater intimate union with God requires one to die. This is not a physical death, but instead we must die to our will and to our self (flesh)!

Going beyond the veil requires us to stop lingering and dancing in front of the veil of God's holy presence. We linger and dance in front of the veil because it excites us and makes our flesh feel good, but this will not bring us close enough to God to know when and where He will move. Lingering and dancing will only allow us to experience the fragrance of where God has been, not where He is going, what He is doing or what He plans to do! (Song of Solomon 5:5-6). Subsequently, we must die more to our flesh and go beyond lingering and dancing in front of the veil because all it does is excite us and appease the flesh.

I will never forget God graciously drawing me into His Secret Place on three separate occasions. During the third encounter in His Secret Place, the Spirit of God asked me "are you seeking the anointing, or God?" As I gathered my thoughts, briefly pausing to ponder the question the Holy Spirit posed before me, I quietly answered "I am seeking God." Promptly, God's Spirit replied, "if you are seeking God, then the anointing should not excite you nor make your flesh feel good." It was at this moment of revelation that I understood my pursuing and chasing God was driven by the presence of where He had excited and pleased my flesh rather than my simply seeking God's face.

At this crossroad and divine moment in eternity, to God be the glory, the Holy Spirit began to teach me to not let my flesh linger in the anointing or the "I feel good *fleshly* syndrome." As a Body of Believers, we must position ourselves through the leading and guiding of the Holy Spirit for the following reasons rather than lingering in the anointing:

- Anointed/anointing carries a function and capability to do something for the kingdom of God. For example, being anointed to preach the gospel (Luke 4:18) causes the anointing to destroy the yoke upon you (Isaiah 10:27). Whenever the anointing shows up, the best thing we can do is simply acknowledge God's anointing and recognize it is there to give us a function and capability to do something for the kingdom of God.

- Anointing can reside in the realms of both spirit and flesh. When the flesh mixes and comes in contact with the anointing, it becomes excited and we can find ourselves experiencing the "I feel good *fleshly* syndrome." Because our flesh is excited and feels good, the anointing's true purpose of carrying a function and capability to do something for the kingdom of God may become lost in the flesh's excitement of the "I feel good *fleshly* syndrome" and emotionalism. The danger of mixing flesh and emotionalism with the anointing is that the anointing can become perverted while emotions lead us away from the very nature and true purpose God provided the anointing for in the first place. Ezekiel 28:14 is a case in point. *"Thou art the anointed cherub that covereth; and I have set thee so: Thou wast upon the holy mountain of God; thou hast walked up and down in the midst of the stones of fire."* Notice that God anointed the cherub to cover and protect. However, his heart became filled with pride, causing him to use the anointing for a purpose other than what God intended (Ezekiel 28:17).

- When we linger in the anointing we will only experience the fragrance of where God *has been*, the presence of *where He was*, witness *what He has already done*, **instead of** *where He is going*, *what He doing* or *what He plans* *to do* (Song of Solomon 5:5-6). By lingering in the anointing and dancing in front of the veil we are only able to see the back parts of God rather than experiencing a divine face-to-face encounter with God (Exodus 33:23).

Chapter 4

EXCITEMENT OF DATING GOD

*"When thou saidst, Seek ye my face; my heart said unto thee, Thy face, L*ORD*, will I seek" (Psalm 27:8).*

W hen we linger and dance in front of the veil, we are basically saying to God that we do not want Him to show us His face and glory, but only want to date Him without making a commitment. We, in all our human foibles, are fine just holding God's hand because the Body of Christ has been spoiled through philosophy and vain deceit, after the religious tradition of men, after the rudiments of the world and not after our Savior, Jesus Christ. Unfortunately, our spoiled condition drives us to seek and become content with what is in God's hands instead of desiring to see His holy face. However, God says "seek my face and that He is a rewarder of them that diligently seek Him."

Oftentimes we seek rewards from God such as His favor, blessings and riches, because although we have seen His hand, we never absorbed or took in the desires of His heart. All the while, God does not want us to be satisfied with what's in His hands. Instead, He desires for us to push His hands aside and seek Him, not just what He can give us. God wants to give us far more. He wants to give those who diligently seek Him the greatest reward imaginable, Himself. God set this pattern when He declared "Fear not, Abram: I am thy shield and thy exceeding great reward" (Genesis 15:1; Psalms 63:1; Hebrew 11:6). What more could a person want and need when God gives Himself as "thy exceeding great reward!"

We have to stop dating and chose to pursue a commitment with God. In the natural world, couples who date tend to have passion, fire and desire towards one another, but not a deep commitment. It is time we purpose in our spirit to diligently seek His face instead of what is in His hands. The greatest blessing any Believer will receive comes from seeking the intimacy of His divine face. This level of true intimacy is only achieved with commitment.

Chapter 5

WHY SEEK HIS FACE?

"Seek the LORD and His strength, seek His face continually" (1 Chronicles 16:11).

Τ he greatest blessing comes not from the hands of God, but from His face in an intimate and committed relationship. That is why God fearfully and wonderfully made us to seek His face. It is only when we lift our inward eyes from our feelings and emotions, the "I feel good *fleshly* syndrome," to gaze upon God, the Creator, that we are sure to meet friendly eyes gazing back at us, for 2 Chronicles 16:9 tells us

"For the eyes of the LORD run to and fro throughout the whole earth, to shew Himself strong in the behalf of them whose heart is perfect toward Him" (2 Chronicles 16:9).

It is only when we divert our eyes from the "I feel good *fleshly* syndrome" and embrace the Father's face that we will realize and see God's loving eyes staring back at us. Further, God's favor flows wherever His face is directed. When we purpose in our spirit for God to show us His glory and diligently seek His face it enables us to tap into His glory, causing the I AM THAT I AM, the Almighty God to turn and incline His divine face toward our face.

Our eyes and God's eyes slowly turn towards us and the two of us become fixated on each other as we lovingly position our face to stare into God's face. It is at this moment that we are able to understand Psalm 32:8 when God decreed that "He will instruct and teach us in the way we should go and guide us with His eye." But to claim this promise we have to be close enough to see Him face-to-face.

When we humble ourselves under the mighty hand of God, He will incline His face toward us (1 Peter 5:6; Psalm 40:1). When we are this close to God we can touch and feel the strength of His face, smell the essence of His love, sense the ambiance of His breath of life and stare deeply into His eyes that reflect boldness, compassion, unity and fullness.

As God inclines and shows us His face, our spirit immediately knows beyond a shadow of doubt that

He only is our rock, our salvation, our fortress and our high tower. Staring into the face of the Almighty, and without God uttering a single word, our heart begins to declare "I shall not be greatly moved!" Continuing to stare, we see in the light of the King's face not just life, but abundant life.

At this moment in eternity, God looks into our eyes lovingly staring at Him and sees His own image reflected in miniature – that is what Psalm 17:8 means when it says "Keep me as the apple of the eye." Once we tap into His glory we can do what He does. This can only happen when we step beyond the veil to seek and touch the face of our God.

The pursuit of God will embrace the labor of bringing our total personality into conformity with God's. In this next season, we can only conform our personality to God when we learn not to tap into our emotions, senses and the "I feel good *fleshly* syndrome," but instead look beyond the lingering and dancing in front of the veil and anointing to embrace and stare into the face of the Almighty God. When we do this we are saying to God we want habitation and not visitation.

Chapter 6

HABITATION OR VISITATION

"And let them make Me a sanctuary; that I may dwell among them" (Exodus 25:8).

Even though God fearfully and wonderfully made us for habitation in His glory, religious traditions have reduced some of us to merely being content with the visitation of His glory. Consequently, these religious-traditional bound Believers have unwittingly settled for just a temporary visit, a brief moment, from the almighty God, believing that habitation or dwelling with the Almighty appears out of reach. Even when our God gently whispers in our ears, "come up hither" and softly tugs at our hearts and spirit, the flesh causes one to linger and dance before the veil because God's glory just paid us a visit.

There is a significant difference between inhabiting and visiting. Habitation occurs when God dwells and abides among His people and they dwell with Him; whereas, visitation happens when God only comes to stay with His people for a short period of time. Do not make a mistake about it, God desires habitation more so than visitation!

How do we know this? Let's look at God's established pattern of habitation. First, we find that God commanded Moses to construct the tabernacle. God told Moses *"and let them make Me a sanctuary; that I may dwell among them"* (Exodus 25:8). Did you catch what God said? "That I may dwell among them."

The tabernacle served as God's original symbol of His dwelling with His people. Next we see that God instructed Nathan to go and tell David, *"Shalt thou build Me a house for Me to dwell in?"* (2 Samuel 7:5). In Ezekiel 43:7 God's established pattern of habitation continue where we witness, "He said unto me, Son of man, the place of my throne and the place of the soles of my feet, where I will dwell in the midst of the children of Israel for ever..." God's established pattern of habitation is further illustrated by the Apostle John.

"And I heard a great voice out of heaven saying, Behold, the tabernacle of God is with men and He will dwell with them and they shall be His

*people and God Himself shall be with them
and be their God" (Revelation 21:3).*

Now let us place God's established pattern of habitation into a present day application to demonstrate the significant difference between habitation and visitation. In order to do this we need to examine two very familiar and fundamental concepts, dating and home.

The dating couple will spend time visiting with each other for short periods of time. Dating normally occurs without a commitment and is reminiscent of lingering and dancing in front of the veil because it is like telling God we do not want Him to show us His face and glory, but only want to date Him and visit for short periods of time without a commitment on our part. However, unlike dating couples who freely enter and leave dating situations as they please, God wants commitment and habitation.

By contrast, habitation or the act of dwelling and abiding with God requires a certain level of commitment and intimacy. Whereas, dating couples may have passion, fire and desire, there is not a deep commitment because true intimacy only results from commitment. That is why it behooves us to stop desiring a dating relationship with God and pursue commitment, intimacy and habitation with

God. When we purposely live this life with God, we come into God's care and dwell in the secret place of the most High and abide under the shadow of the Almighty (Psalm 91:1).

Let us look at the second fundamental concept, home, to further understand the significant difference between habitation and visitation. We have all had visitors stay in our homes and while we generally look forward to the visit, we also know they will only stay for a short period of time. In preparation for the visitors we normally ensure the house is clean and in good order, linens are washed and that there is plenty of food to eat. We do whatever is necessary to make our guests feel comfortable. During their visit, although we tolerate certain quirks and mannerisms the visitors may have, we normally do not let them have complete run of the home or total access to every room. There are also certain privileges and rights enjoyed by the occupants of the home that are not available to the guests. Once the visit is over, we say our goodbyes and the visitors finally leave and our lives and homes go back to normal.

This is not the case, however, with other occupants in your home. It is difficult to ignore them because unlike visitors, they are not just here temporarily, but dwell in the home permanently. Subsequently, everything about our life and home now involves someone else and their life. This relationship causes us to seek the opinions and advice of the other occupants because of their permanent residency in areas we would never do with visitors. Their dwelling or living in the home gives them certain privileges and rights that visitors do not enjoy. For instance, home occupants have complete access to every room in the home and freely roam from room to room. Furthermore, having other occupants dwelling in the home causes us to involve them in the order of the home and its function.

The reality is that Almighty God does not just want visitations for short periods of time. Our Father does not want us to just make a few modest, comfortable and tolerable adjustments to our lives while waiting for the visit to end. God wants to be an occupant, dwelling and living together beside us. He wants to exercise the privileges and rights that come with occupancy including involving Him in our lives and seeking His advice because we abide under the shadow of the Almighty.

We must earnestly embrace the concept that visitation from God is nothing like His habitation among us. As nice as it is, we should not readily seek another visitation from God. We need habitation much more than visitation! How many times has God visited us and afterwards we strayed back to where we were before the divine visitation occurred?

This backsliding is the reason we desperately need to yearn for God to dwell among us and for us to abide under the shadow of the Almighty. We need to dwell with Him and He with us. We need to live with His constant abiding presence in our lives. Why settle for a short visit when God offers habitation? We should not any longer consider lingering and dancing before the veil a viable option to experience the fullness of the King of Glory because at best it only provides a brief visitation from God. Habitation occurs when we go beyond the veil.

We need to embrace and transform our mind into realizing that God's habitation is better than His visitation:

"The Lord is my strength and song, and He is become my salvation: He is my God, and I will prepare Him an habitation; my father's God, and I will exalt him" (Exodus 15:2).

"Thou in thy mercy hast led forth the people which thou hast redeemed: thou hast guided

them in thy strength unto thy holy habitation"
(Exodus 15:13).

"Be thou my strong habitation, whereunto I
may continually resort: thou hast given commandment to save me; for thou art my rock
and my fortress" (Psalm 71:3).

"Because thou hast made the LORD, which is
my refuge, even the most High, thy habitation; There shall no evil befall thee, neither
shall any plague come nigh thy dwelling"
(Psalm 91:9-10).

"And I will pray the Father, and he shall give
you another Comforter, that he may abide with
you forever; Even the Spirit of truth; whom
the world cannot receive, because it seeth
Him not, neither knoweth Him: but ye know
Him; for He dwelleth with you, and shall be
in you" (John 14:16-17).

Chapter 7

DO NOT TURN GOD'S GLORY INTO SHAME

"O ye sons of men, how long will ye turn My glory into shame? How long will ye love vanity and seek after leasing (lying; falsehoods)? Selah" Psalm 4:2.

J esus Christ tells us in John 4:23-24 that God is a Spirit and we must worship Him in spirit and in truth. Sadly, our worship is far removed from worshipping God in this manner. Oftentimes, we engage in ***presumptuous*** and ***pretentious*** worship, full of vanity and vain words which so easily beset us, which we then try to present to God as true worship and praise.

God's purpose is to reveal Himself through the act of true worship that is God focused and centered and lasts throughout all eternity. Presumptuous and pretentious worship fades just as quickly as it goes up because it focuses on glorifying the flesh, dressing it in presumed glory, "I feel good *fleshly* syndrome," but finds itself grounded in vanity. God desires praise and worship that does not seek its own merit but rather the face and Heart of God to promote His glory to fill the temple with His glory.

Presumptuous and pretentious worship is an act of offering strange incense and fire to God, then expecting God not only to be thrilled and happy with it, but to accept it as worshipping Him in spirit and in truth. Ask Nadab and Abihu, the sons of Aaron about how God feels about offering strange fire to Him (Leviticus 10:1).

These sons of Aaron approached God to worship Him not in spirit and in truth, but instead offered presumptuous and pretentious worship, strange fire, before the Lord. Their presumptuous and pretentious worship was so full of vanity and vain words that they failed to seek the Heart of God but acted in the "I feel good *fleshly* syndrome" which pleased their flesh and not God. At best, presumptuous and pretentious worship attempts to use carnal means to kindle fires of true devotion and praise. But God is not mocked. He wants all those who come near Him to glorify and worship Him in spirit and in truth.

Worshipping in spirit and in truth, unlike presumptuous and pretentious worship, is a deliberate, steady focused time with the Father, not on our terms, but on the Father's terms. God desires this type of worship because it:

- Causes the worshipper to expect a divine encounter with Him and to seek His face
- Places the worshipper under God's loving care so the Lord can shape the character and mold the heart of the worshipper
- Develops in the worshipper a focused relationship of faith, obedience, trust and dependency with God
- Leads the worshipper to acknowledge God's activity and work in the worshipper's life
- Directs the life of the worshipper into the midst and heart of His will

Chapter 8

SUFFERING FOR GOD'S GRACE AND GLORY

"But the God of all grace, who hath called us unto His eternal glory by Christ Jesus, after that ye have suffered a while, make you perfect, establish, strengthen, settle you" (1 Peter 5:10).

Many Believers either fail to realize or do not want to realize that God's word says we will suffer and face persecution for His glory. There are three foundational scriptures we must fully comprehend in order to grasp the significance of suffering for God's grace and glory.

"For I reckon that the sufferings of this present time are not worthy to be compared with the glory which shall be revealed in us" (Romans 8:18).

"And He said unto me, My grace is sufficient for thee: for my strength is made perfect in weakness. Most gladly therefore will I rather glory in my infirmities, that the power of Christ may rest upon me" (2 Corinthians 12:9).

"Beloved, think it not strange concerning the fiery trial which is to try you, as though some strange thing happened unto you. But rejoice, inasmuch as ye are partakers of Christ's sufferings; that, when His glory shall be revealed, ye may be glad also with exceeding joy. Yet if any man suffer as a Christian, let him not be ashamed; but let him glorify God on this behalf "(1 Peter 4:12-13, 16).

The word of God is clear regarding suffering, saying that we will all suffer and face tribulations. As a Body of Believers we tend to look at suffering through our natural eyes rather than view it from the perspective of our eternal Father.

Why does the word of God clearly say in 2 Corinthians 4:17 that our affliction is light and but for a moment, while James 1:2 goes on to tell us to count it all joy when we fall into divers temptations? The word further goes on to say we glory in our suffering.

When we are suffering due to difficult and harsh circumstances, whether it be divorce, loss of a job, death of a loved one, financial ruin or whatever the circumstances may be, all we tend to feel is that pain, discomfort, chaos, lack of hope and the loss of joy. But the word of God says to rejoice and count it all joy! Unfortunately, we focus on the natural, what our flesh feels, what our eyes see and what our ears hear, even though Acts 14:22 encourages us that we must through much tribulation enter into the kingdom of God.

Notice that the scripture does not state "some tribulation," but says we enter in through "much tribulation." We need to understand how to handle and glory in suffering. Why does the word of God call for us to suffer, and how should we respond to it?

We as a Body of Believers must glory in suffering. To do so we must concentrate on four specific areas:

- Stop running from suffering
- Just bear suffering
- Glory in suffering
- Benefits of suffering

Stop Running From Suffering
"Reproach hath broken my heart; and I am full of heaviness: and I looked for some to take

*pity, but there was none; and for comforters,
but I found none" (Psalm 69:20).*

When we tend to look at our suffering, our pain, our diseases, our sicknesses or whatever is going on in the present – the here and now, our instincts are to run away from it. But, why should we stop running from suffering? Simply put, what the eternal Father wants to do in the midst of our suffering is to reveal His glory in and through us.

The eternal Father wants to raise us up so that the Body of Christ and non-believers can witness what His awesome glory and spiritual might can do. Unfortunately, we tend to run from suffering rather than running to it. When we refuse to embrace suffering, the eternal Father cannot reveal His glory in us. When we run from suffering we are actually running from the eternal Father! We are running to our pain, hurt, anxiety, distress, despair, persecution and a whole host of troubles and sorrows.

We tend to embrace these circumstances, then wonder why we are in this predicament and these circumstances prevail and one trial after another comes our way. The reason is we are running away from suffering rather than embracing it. Furthermore, it seems like when most of us are experiencing heaviness and manifold temptations, we look for someone to pity us.

We quickly embrace our pity party and settle down in the midst of our suffering, earnestly looking for someone to pat us on the back and tell us everything will be alright, just hang in there and things will get better. But this pity party just makes the circumstances worse because the individuals we turn to for sympathy and encouragement are miserable comforters. It is at this precise moment that we should turn away from the pity parties and those who are babying us and fully turn our heart and attention to our Lord Jesus Christ.

We need to realize in the midst of our troubles there are some people who never conquered and came out of their own troubles and trials, therefore, they cannot help us. We instead need to look for someone who survived troubles and harsh circumstances and came out as more than a conqueror. We need to embrace these individuals so that they can, through the power and strength of the Holy Spirit show us how to come out. So why do we run to people who cannot help us out of our trials and tribulations? They are deep in the mire and in the midst of trials and tribulations themselves and all they can tell us is to cry it out. They even begin to cry with us.

We have a great time crying during our pity party and have only the taste of salty tears to comfort and help us. Unfortunately, the pity partiers do not have a word of hope or life to feed our spirit. Consequently, we end up discovering that we do not have anything, not even the word of God or His power to comfort and bring us out of the suffering. This is why we must stop running from suffering and embrace it.

When we embrace the suffering we will find the Almighty God, the Lord Jesus Christ and the Holy Spirit waiting for us in the very center of the trouble and suffering. It is in the midst of this suffering that the Lord Jesus Christ gives rest and comfort to those who are heavy laden and come unto Him. When we embrace suffering we will quickly come to know the Lord as a refuge, our shield, a fortress and a rock and find rest for our souls. It is an amazing thing to be in the midst of suffering while finding rest and comfort because of the Lord Jesus Christ.

There is something about the King of Glory where our Lord shows us the deepness and depth of His heart and His love when we are in the midst of our suffering. It is at this point that we begin to trust and depend on the Lord who is our present help in times of trouble. In the midst of our suffering we need to hold on to our Lord Jesus Christ's right hand and rely on the Holy Spirit's might and strength. We should call out to the Lord, acknowledging to Him that we cannot make it without His being on our side and tell Him we need to see more of Him in order to survive the suffering. We need to lean on, begin to trust and allow Him to lead and guide us. When we do this the Lord will rise up in the midst of our circumstances and open His heart to us as we begin to realize we are after His heart.

The Lord, out of eternity, then begins to whisper *"this is a person who trusts Me, this is a person who believes in Me, this is a person who pushes suffering, trials and tribulation aside, this is a person who wants to live with Me, and this is a person who wants Me as the Lord of their life."* As a result, the Lord Jesus Christ begins to lift us up so that we can just bear suffering.

Just Bear Suffering

> *"There hath no temptation taken you but such as is common to man: but God is faithful, who will not suffer you to be tempted above that ye are able; but will with the temptation also make a way to escape, that ye may be able to bear it" (1 Corinthians 10:13).*

The second specific area we must concentrate on in order to glory in suffering is to bear suffering according to the formula in 1 Corinthians 10:13. There is not any temptation taken us but such as is common to man and God will not allow us to be tempted above what we are able to bear. The first thing we need to understand is that the trials, tribulations and circumstances we are experiencing are not unique to us.

As a matter of fact, the word of God in 1 Peter 4:12 boldly tells us to "think it not strange concerning the fiery trial which is to try us, as though some strange thing happened unto us." The next time you face trials, tribulations and suffering, just look around and you will find someone who has gone through that same trial and tribulation.

There are not new trials, what is new is how we handle them. Do we embrace the suffering and not look at our pain and hurt? We just need to remember and place deep in our heart that God is faithful and will not suffer (allow) us to be tempted above that we are able to bear! In the midst of our suffering we really need to meditate on these words and allow them to enter our spirit. We must come to the realization that since God allows the suffering to come into our life, we need to wholeheartedly blurt out the following to the King of Glory when faced with suffering.

Proclamation

"Oh God you allowed this suffering and trial, therefore You must have a divine purpose in mind. There must be a need for the trial and tribulation. God, just show me what You are trying to do in and through my life. God, since you allowed this trial and tribulation it must mean that I can bear it!"

If we could not bear the pain and suffering, then the Almighty would not allow it to enter our life, but would shield and protect us from it. Subsequently, in the midst of our suffering there must be something we need to know and understand. That something is to seek the face of the King of Glory, to step into the secret place of the Most High, abide under the shadow of the Almighty and sit down in His presence while He speaks and reveals Himself to us.

When we do this, we will realize that suffering is a meeting place where we can step into the secret place of the Most High where the worst of us and the best of God come together and we come away with the best of God upon us. In the secret place of the Most High,

His love, grace, presence and glory will alleviate our pain and turn our attention away from our suffering to the Almighty, I AM THAT I AM. Further, we can step out of the secret place of the Most High with boldness on us, full of authority and power.

When we look back on our trials and tribulations, we can righteously state that although we were in the midst of suffering, God's grace is sufficient. His power kept us and He brought us through. Furthermore, we will not only say the Almighty brought us through our suffering, but that in it all He revealed His presence, grace, mercy, love and the depths of His heart to us. When we stand firm in the word and bear the suffering we will soon realize that the power of Christ rests upon us and we shall not die, but live and declare the works of the LORD. That is why it is extremely important to stop running from suffering. Just bear it and glory in suffering. Glory in suffering is the third specific area we must concentrate on.

Glory in Suffering

   "For I reckon that the sufferings of this present time are not worthy to be compared with the glory which shall be revealed in us" *(Romans 8:18).*

51

"For our light affliction, which is but for a moment, worketh for us a far more exceeding and eternal weight of glory" (2 Corinthians 4:17).

"Yet if any man suffer as a Christian, let him not be ashamed; but let him glorify God on this behalf" (1 Peter 4:16).

We need to heed what the word of God tells us and encourages us about glorying in suffering. The scriptures remind us that our affliction only exists for a moment when laid alongside of eternity and is considered but a light thing compared with the eternal weight of glory one receives for sufferings. Because of this, we should not be ashamed of our suffering because our eternal Father wants to reveal His glory in us through the suffering. Also, our glory in suffering makes the Lord Jesus Christ known and gives life to others. Therefore, we should glory in our sufferings and count them as joy while we win others to the Lord Jesus Christ and witness His abundant grace save many souls, causing them to give more praise to the glory of God.

We must learn a vital lesson from the prophet Jeremiah. Time and time again, God sent Jeremiah to the nation of Israel, yet they neither hearkened nor inclined their ear but continuously walked in the counsels and in the imagination of their evil heart and went backward and not forward. As a matter of fact, the very people God sent Jeremiah to help were stubborn and did not want to hear the truth because to do so would require them to change. They were so hardened to doing God's will that the people eventually plotted to kill Jeremiah. Their rejection, which Jeremiah knew would eventually bring the wrath of God upon them caused him to become sorrowful and to focus on his pain and sorrow. He stated "woe is me for my hurt and my wound is grievous."

When he penned this verse, Jeremiah was wrapped up in his suffering. However, somewhere in his suffering Jeremiah remembered the Lord. He also remembered that our affliction is light and but for a moment, and to count it all joy when we fall into divers temptations. As a result, Jeremiah came to himself and began to realize that he served a mighty God; a God that is much larger than the stubborn and stiff-necked people of the nation of Israel. Subsequently, Jeremiah shouted "*I said, truly this is a grief and I must bear it!*" In other words, Jeremiah was saying I realize this is pain and sorrow. I realize my wound is grievous, but now I must bear it. Jeremiah realized that when he bore the suffering, he would meet the King of Glory and come into the presence of the eternal Father and the Lord Jesus Christ.

We can also learn a lesson from Paul, who had a thorn in the flesh, the messenger of Satan to buffet him. Paul besought the Lord three times for this thorn to depart from him. However, the Lord said unto Paul *My grace is sufficient for thee: for my strength is made perfect in weakness.* What the Lord was really saying to Paul was *"Paul listen to Me, just listen to Me, it is My grace that will keep you. It is My grace that will protect you. It is My grace that will preserve you from all trials, tribulations, hurts and dangers. It is because of My grace that you will learn more about My presence."*

Paul understood the sufficiency of the Lord's grace. It is noteworthy to realize that Paul wanted God's presence, grace, power and strength working in him because he knew if he would just bear and glory in suffering, the Lord would make him perfect. As a body of Believers, we too must realize our eternal Father blesses us like He did Paul and His strength is made perfect in our weakness. Our weakness causes us to seek the Lord, drives us into His presence and brings fresh intimacy with and glory to the Almighty God.

Paul realized the glory the Lord wanted to reveal in and through his life was far greater than any suffering he would encounter. That is why Paul gladly said he will glory in his infirmities. It is important for us to understand why Paul was so adamant about glorying in his infirmities. It is because the following four things will happen when we stop running from and embrace, bear and glory in our suffering to look and see what God wants to do in and through our life.

- Power of Christ rest upon us
- Spirit of glory and of God will rest upon us
- Tribulations will produce patience and patience, hope
- Lord Jesus Christ shall lift up our head above our enemies

Power of Christ Rests Upon Us

First, when we gladly glory in our infirmities, the power of Christ can rest upon us as recorded in 2 Corinthians 12:9. We need to remember and keep fresh in our mind that our infirmities, as well as the years of the right hand of the most High holding our right hand, saying unto thee, *"Fear not; I will help thee."* Our mind should focus on this promise of help as we realize the Almighty is holding our right hand. When we are in the midst of troubles, trials and tribulations, the Lord is always there to hold our right hand, to comfort, to give rest and to deliver us.

Spirit of Glory and of God Will Rest Upon Us

The second thing that happens to us when we stop running from suffering and just bear and glory in it is found in 1 Peter 4:14 – the Spirit of glory and of God will rest upon us. Therefore, when we begin to just bear the suffering, the power of God will rest upon us. When we begin to bear our suffering the Spirit of glory and of God will also rest upon us.

Tribulations Will Produce Patience and Patience, Hope

Third, when we just bear our suffering and glory in tribulations, they will produce patience and patience, hope. It is the Lord's desire to uphold us according to His word so that we may live and hope makes us unashamed because the love of God is poured out in our heart as found in Psalm 119:116 and Romans 5:3-5. Subsequently, we need to understand what hope really means. Simply put, hope is our expectation in God! Furthermore, our soul should wait only upon God, for our expectation is from Him.

We just need to bear our suffering and during every moment in suffering we must have expectancy from the Lord. Further, we need to remember that faith is the substance of things hoped for, the evidence of things not seen. The world views and believes hope to be a 50–50 proposition, in other words, it may or may not happen. But, our God views hope as a certainty of fulfillment, a strong and confident expectation, an assurance and a guarantee because hope is coupled with faith.

Let us look closely at hope. We know that everyone will experience trials and tribulations, but when we have hope, we have a great expectancy from the Lord. Swallowed up in this expectancy is the overwhelming belief that the Lord knows how to deliver the godly out of temptations (2 Peter 2:9). The mistake we sometimes make in the midst of our trials, tribulations and suffering is to try to figure our own way out. Once we think we have developed a foolproof plan, we go to the Lord, asking Him to sanction it.

We tend to not only present our plan to the Lord, but we fool heartedly tell the Lord what the problem is and then tell Him how He should deliver us from the problem. We need to change this mindset and approach the Lord with the expectation that He knows precisely how to, when to, and that He will deliver us out of temptations and afflictions.

We need to realize the Lord does not need our feeble help in delivering us out of temptations and afflictions. But, what the Lord does require is that we hope or have an expectation in God and couple our hope with faith. Instead of telling the Lord how to deliver us out of temptations, we just need to depend, lean on and believe in the Lord. In the day of our trouble we should seek and call upon the Lord with great assurance, expecting Him to answer and deliver us out of all temptations. Surely there is an end! For the Lord's thoughts toward us are of peace and not of evil to give us an expected end and our expectation shall not be cut off. Furthermore, we should not let the Lord's mode of deliverance out of our temptations and afflictions concern us.

The Lord strong and mighty only wants us to trust in Him with all our heart and lean not unto our own understanding. In times of troubles and suffering, we should stir up and bury Psalm 54:7 deep in our heart and spirit.

"For He hath delivered me out of all trouble: and mine eye hath seen His desire upon mine enemies" (Psalm 54:7).

What a blessed assurance of hope and expectancy, knowing that we serve the Lord of hosts, the King of Glory, who not only knows how to deliver us out of temptations but delivers us out of not some, but all trouble.

"Many are the afflictions of the righteous. But God has delivered him out of them all" (Psalm 34:19).

Regardless of the afflictions, temptations, trials, tribulations and problems we face, our Lord is an ever present help in time of trouble and will surely make haste to deliver and help us. When we just bear our suffering and glory in tribulations it causes us to have a strong confidence and an assured expectation that the Lord will deliver us out of all our temptations.

"For in the time of trouble He shall hide me in His pavilion: in the secret of His tabernacle shall He hide me; He shall set me up upon a rock. And now shall mine head be lifted up above my enemies round about me: therefore will I offer in His tabernacle sacrifices of joy: I will sing, yea, I will sing praises unto the Lord" (Psalm 27:5-6).

"He that dwelleth in the secret place of the most High shall abide under the shadow of the Almighty" (Psalm 91:1).

When you abide under the shadow of the Almighty, God's shadow is so immense that wherever the Lord's shadow goes, we shall closely follow Him under the cover of His shadow. This means that the Lord's shadow will cover us from those fiery darts of the wicked and prevent those trials and tribulations from overwhelming us. The Lord wants to hide us in the secret of His tabernacle and set us upon a rock. We know that this Rock is the Lord Jesus Christ. The Almighty set us upon the rock so the power of Christ, the Spirit of glory and the Spirit of God may rest upon us as we stop running from and just bear and glory in suffering.

Lord Shall Lift Up Our Head Above Our Enemies

The fourth and final thing that happens when we stop running from our suffering and embrace it, looking to see what God wants to do in and through our life, is that the Lord shall lift up our head above our enemies. This means that as we embrace, endure and bear suffering, although those light afflictions may come for a moment, when we lean on and trust in the Lord, He will rise us up and lift our head above our enemies that are all around us. The Lord will lift us up to a new dimension in Him where He will hide us in the secret of His presence. Realize if you will, in the secret of His presence there is nothing that can come against you! In the secret of His presence we will only experience and see God the Father, God the Son and God the Holy Spirit in addition to all the host of heaven.

This is what is in the secret of His presence! The Lord wants us to come into the secret of His presence, enjoying the same thing the Father, the Son and the Holy Spirit see. Subsequently, in the secret of His presence as He lifts up our head, our eyes are diverted from our circumstances and riveted on the Father, the Son and the Holy Spirit, enabling us to stand tall above those trials, tribulations, problems, diseases, sicknesses and sufferings.

Our tribulations and sufferings are now down in the valley of the shadow of death. But, if we fail to embrace our suffering and keep our focus attuned to our trials, tribulations and problems, we will find ourselves stuck in the valley along with them. That is why some of us cannot find our healing and are unable to experience liberty. That is why deliverance escapes some of us and we are forced to continuously endure the pain, hurt and turmoil that seemingly goes on forever and ever. We need to get out of the valley of the shadow of death! As long as we are in the valley of the shadow of death, we are saying to pain, hurt and turmoil that they are welcome to come and take over our life.

As a result, it is crucial for us to embrace Psalm 27:5-6 so that we do not remain down in the valley of the shadow of death any longer with that pain, hurt and turmoil. Our heads are lifted up and we boldly stand on the mountaintop under the shadow of the Almighty. It is here, under the protective shadow of the Almighty that we can take power, authority and dominion over our trials, tribulations, pain, hurt, turmoil and whatever else is wreaking havoc in our life. It is under the shadow of the Almighty that we can speak to our trials and tribulations and command them to leave because we serve a mighty God that delivers us from all our troubles and afflictions.

When the Lord has lifted our heads above our enemies all around us and we have learned to take power, authority and dominion over our pain, hurt and turmoil, as we glory in tribulations the Lord can send us to rescue and bring others out of the valley of the shadow of death. We can go into the valley under the full protection and shadow of the Almighty with the power of Christ resting upon us, saturated in the authority of the Lord Jesus Christ and confident in our God-given dominion to righteously and boldly proclaim deliverance to the captives, the recovering of sight to the blind and set at liberty them that are bruised.

We must fully realize that the Lord Jesus Christ created each of us for His good works with the power of Christ, the Spirit of glory and the Spirit of God resting upon us in order to speak life and that people might have it more abundantly. This is why it is extremely important for us to embrace, bear and glory in suffering. In times of trouble, when faced with turmoil, pain, hurt and tribulations, just remember we are the Lord Jesus Christ's workmanship and created for His good works. It behooves us to reflect and meditate on the following verses.

"For we are His workmanship, created in Christ Jesus unto good works, which God hath before ordained that we should walk in them" (Ephesians 2:10).

"Being confident of this very thing, that He which hath begun a good work in you will perform it until the day of Jesus Christ" (Philippians 1:6).

*"I shall not die, but live and declare the works
of the Lord" (Psalm 118:17).*

We must live to declare the Lord Jesus Christ's
goodness and how His power keeps us. We need to
live in order to proclaim how the Lord delivered us
out of all our afflictions and problems. We must live to
enable the Lord Jesus Christ to use us to bring others
out the valley of the shadow of death. We must live
to fill the earth with the glory of God. We must live to
boldly proclaim the name and gospel of Jesus Christ.

Benefits of Suffering
*"But the God of all grace, who hath called us
unto His eternal glory by Christ Jesus, after
that ye have suffered a while, make you perfect,
establish, strengthen, settle you" (1 Peter 5:10).*

We have learned the importance of stopping our
running from suffering and why we should embrace
it, as well as bear and glory in suffering. Now let us
examine the fourth and final specific area, the benefits
of suffering that we must concentrate on. These four
benefits are found in 1 Peter 5:10. After, not before
we have suffered, the Lord will:

- Make us perfect

- Establish us
- Strengthen us
- Settle us

Make Us Perfect

After we stop running from and embrace, just bear and glory in suffering, the Lord makes us perfect. The word perfect means complete, to lack nothing, to know the Lord is our shepherd and we shall not want. What the Lord wants to do when He says He will make us perfect is to give us all the provisions we need. In 1 Corinthians 10:13 it states that *"God is faithful, who will not suffer you to be tempted above that ye are able; but will with the temptation also make a way to escape, that ye may be able to bear it."* The Lord Jesus Christ will provide us with all the necessary provisions to enable us to bear the temptations – His grace that is more than sufficient. Further, we must get it in our spirit that God wants to make all grace abound toward us so that we will have sufficiency in all areas in great abundance.

Establish Us

The second benefit is the Lord will establish us. Establish means to place firmly or fix securely in position. In other words, the Lord wants to firmly put us in a place – the secret place of the most High God!

"Thou shalt hide them in the secret of thy presence from the pride of man: thou shalt keep them secretly in a pavilion from the strife of tongues" (Psalm 31:20).

The Lord will establish us by not allowing the pride of man (all the backbiting, trauma, plotting and conniving that goes on) to bring us down and entrap us in the valley of the shadow of death. This is because the Lord will firmly and securely establish us in the secret of His presence from the pride of man and will keep and protect us in the secret of His pavilion.

Strengthen Us

The third benefit is we are able to be strengthened by the Lord. We need to realize that the Lord's grace is sufficient and His strength is made perfect in our weakness. A case in point is the prophet Elijah, who under the hand and strength of the Lord ran and arrived at the entrance of Jezreel before King Ahab did. This is very significant when one considers that to accomplish this, Elijah had to run a distance of over 30 miles at a faster speed than a chariot drawn by fast horses. What the Lord wants us to know is to relay on His strength and might and not our own because our flesh will fail us in times of trouble, but God is the strength of our heart and portion for evermore.

It is the Lord who gives power to the faint and to them that do not have might, He increases their strength. After we embrace, just bear and glory in suffering, the Lord will renew our strength because we are waiting on Him. The most vigorous and powerful men may faint under strain and utterly fall, but those who wait on the Lord shall renew their strength, mount up with wings as eagles, run and not be weary and walk and not faint. This is what the strength of the Lord will do for us. The Lord Jesus Christ is our ultimate source of strength and wisdom. Our Lord is the infinite wellspring of both the necessary strategies for life and navigating the waters of troubled times. Only our Lord Jesus Christ is our vast eternal reservoir of our true strength and might.

The eternal Father does not want us to face troubled times in our own strength. He alone will inspire us to do what we need to do and will fill us with the amount of strength and might of the Holy Spirit equal to the task He calls us to do in order to accomplish His will, purpose and good works.

"Then He answered and spake unto me, saying, This is the word of the Lord unto Zerubbabel, saying, Not by might, nor by power, but by My Spirit, saith the LORD of hosts" (Zechariah 4:6).

"That He would grant you, according to the riches of His glory, to be strengthened with might by His Spirit in the inner man" (Ephesians 3:16).

"I can do all things through Christ which strengtheneth me" (Philippians 4:13).

"Strengthened with all might, according to His glorious power, unto all patience and long-suffering with joyfulness" (Colossians 1:11).

These scriptures reinforce that it is not through our strength and might, but through the power, might and strength of the Spirit of God that the Lord's strength is made perfect in our weakness so we can do His good works. Further, the Lord strengthens us so that we can resist temptation. We must clearly understand that the only reason we can do all things is through Jesus Christ, who strengthens us. This means that the true source of power is not by might, nor by human power, but by the Holy Spirit's anointing. This should reassure us that despite pain, hurt, turmoil, troubles, trials and tribulations, these harsh circumstances will not hinder our good works in the Lord because we have stopped running from and embraced, then just bared and gloried in suffering.

Oftentimes we hear people quote the last part of Nehemiah 8:10, *"the joy of the Lord is your strength."* But, have we ever taken the time to meditate on and contemplate what this scripture truly means to us, especially when we face suffering? Joy is important because the joy of the Lord is our strength! The Joy of the Lord produces the strength that we desperately need to fight the good fight of faith. Unfortunately, many in the Body of Christ struggle to fight the good fight of faith because they have lost their joy and do not depend on the joy of the Lord. This statement is worth repeating. "They have lost their joy and do not depend on the joy of the Lord."

There is a difference between our joy and the joy of the Lord. Our joy is laced with feelings, cheerfulness and happy emotions and the expression or display of these emotions. Our joy fades whenever we are unhappy or faced with some type of dissatisfaction and displeasure in life. We oftentimes lose our joy and struggle in life when we are confronted with trials, tribulations, problems and suffering. However, the joy of the Lord is not dependent on feelings, happiness or cheerfulness.

The joy of the Lord emanates from His being, all that He is and is the fruit of the Spirit. Troubles on every side, distresses, perplexities, persecutions and sufferings do not hamper or dissuade the joy of the Lord. The joy of the Lord remains unchanged and powerful. The joy of the Lord can only give us strength when we possess it. As a matter of fact, the God of hope wants to fill us with all joy and peace so that we may abound in hope through the power of the Holy Ghost (Romans 15:13). The Lord fills us with His joy so that it can remain in us, causing our joy to be full despite tribulations and suffering. His joy fills us with comfort and we overflow with His joy. Therefore, the joy of the Lord gives us strength and we can rejoice with joy unspeakable and full of glory in the midst of our suffering. Further, the joy of the Lord gives us the necessary strength to have great boldness and fearless confidence to stop running from and embrace, just bear and glory in suffering.

Settle Us

The fourth benefit we receive after we stop running from and embrace, just bear and glory in suffering, is the Lord will settle us. Settle means to bring order. The Lord wants to bring order into our life and bring us to a place where there is rest in our life.

> *"Come unto Me, all ye that labour and are heavy laden and I will give you rest. Take my yoke upon you and learn of me: for I am meek and lowly in heart: and ye shall find rest unto your souls. For My yoke is easy and my burden is light" (Matthew 11:28-30).*

The Lord wants to settle us so we may know rest in the midst of our trials, tribulations and suffering. We must change our mindset and run to the Lord Jesus Christ from whence comes all our help and realize the Lord is an ever present help in our times of trouble. In other words, the Lord will never leave nor forsake us in time of trouble. When we seek Him in the day of our trouble, the Lord will comfort our soul, for the eyes of the Lord are over the righteous and His ears are open unto their cries and prayers.

The Lord hears the cry of the righteous and delivers them out of all their troubles. Our trust, belief and reliance in the Lord and His word will cause us to hope, which is our comfort in our affliction, for God's word will give us life. Therefore, when we find ourselves facing trials, tribulations and suffering, the first thing we need to do is to embrace our suffering, which will enable us to find the Lord Jesus Christ in the very midst. Then we should proclaim, "Lord I know you allowed suffering in my life for a reason, now show me how You want to reveal Yourself in my life. Show me Your holy presence. Show me your glory" and He will.

Chapter 9

IT IS ALL A MIND THING

"And be not conformed to this world: but be ye transformed by the renewing of your mind, that ye may prove what is that good and acceptable and perfect will of God" (Romans 12:2).

"Let this mind be in you, which was also in Christ Jesus" (Philippians 2:5).

The one thing the word of God tells us is that we can expect trials and tribulations and that throughout our life we will face situations and run into strongholds and burdens. What matters is how we handle those trials, situations and strongholds. *It is all a mind thing!*

Think about what the word of God says in Romans 12:2 and Philippians 2:5. It is a mind thing how we handle trials. It is an attitude how we cope with tribulations. It is a way of thinking how we deal with our situations. It is what is in our mind that causes us to press through and pull down strongholds. How we choose to deal with trials, tribulations and situations will bring our deliverance and healing, enabling us to break those yokes and chains. So let this mind be in you which was also in Christ Jesus. *It is all a mind thing!*

A review of Paul and Silas' imprisonment in Acts 16, helps us to fully understand this. The Holy Spirit directed Paul and Silas not to go into Bithynia to preach the word but instead a vision appeared to Paul of a man of Macedonia who stood praying and saying, *"Come over into Macedonia and help us."* After seeing the vision the two of them immediately endeavored to go into Macedonia, assuredly gathering that the Lord had called them to preach the gospel in Macedonia.

When Paul and Silas arrived in Macedonia they went to Lydia, a seller of purple, of the city of Thyatira, who worshipped God. Paul and Silas prayed with Lydia and baptized her and her household. Afterwards Paul and Silas encountered a certain damsel possessed with a spirit of divination. She followed them and taunted Paul and Silas for many days. Finally, Paul being grieved turned and said to the spirit *"I command thee in the name of Jesus Christ to come out of her"* and the spirit came out the same hour. Unfortunately, this episode irritated her masters because all hope of their gain was gone. In other words, they were losing money. Subsequently, they caught and brought Paul and Silas before the rulers in the marketplace. The rulers (magistrates) ordered Paul and Silas to be beaten with many stripes.

We can imagine how these many stripes caused Paul and Silas to suffer grievous, open and bloody wounds. As if these wounds were not enough, the magistrates cast them into prison and charged the jailer to keep Paul and Silas safe. In turn, the jailer thrust Paul and Silas into the inner prison and put their feet in stocks. The stocks were designed to raise their feet off the ground and keep them from moving about. The inner prison was an underground dungeon in utter darkness. Think about if we were Paul and Silas. The Spirit of the living God directs us to a place to preach the gospel and we eagerly go to do the Lord's work, only to find ourselves beaten and thrown into a dark dungeon.

Despite their harsh treatment, at midnight Paul and Silas prayed and sang praises unto God and the prisoners heard them. We may wonder what motivated Paul and Silas to pray and sang praises at this late hour with their feet in stocks, bleeding from their many wounds and immersed in darkness. What was going through their minds to cause them to praise and focus on God? While we do not know what they were praying and singing, rest assured Paul and Silas were not saying *"oh woe is me, or woe my hurt, I was just beaten with many stripes almost to the point of death, I am hurting, I am in deep trouble."* On the contrary, Paul and Silas kept the Lord God before their faces to such an extent that all they could see at that precise moment was God Himself. *It is all a mind thing!*

We should also imagine that Paul and Silas were praying and singing five particular noteworthy songs of praise (a prayer of protection, a prayer of dependency, a prayer of trust, a prayer of praise and a prayer of promised help) that changed the atmosphere, opened the windows of heaven and inspired the Spirit of the Lord to arise in the midst and fill the darkness of the dungeon with the glory of God. *It is all a mind thing!*

A Prayer of Protection

> *"And behold, I am with thee and will keep thee in all places whither thou goest and will bring thee again into this land; for I will not leave thee, until I have done that which I have spoken of thee" (Genesis 28:15).*

"There shall not any man be able to stand before thee all the days of thy life; as I was with Moses, so I will be with thee: I will not fail thee, nor forsake thee" (Joshua 1:5).

"Have not I commanded thee: Be strong and of a good courage: be not afraid, neither be thou dismayed: for the LORD thy God is with thee whithersoever thou goest" (Joshua 1:9).

"Let your conversation be without covetousness; and be content with such things as ye have for He hath said, I will never leave thee, nor forsake thee" (Hebrews 13:5).

Paul and Silas remembered the Lord and what He said in His word. What Paul and Silas were praying and singing about was that the Almighty would keep them in every place they went and never leave nor forsake them. Paul and Silas, despite their harsh conditions and the darkness of the dungeon, boldly prayed and sang that God was with them. In their mind and heart, they knew the Lord Almighty was there in prison with and sitting next to them. Paul and Silas were confident that the Lord would keep them in every place that they went and all they had to do was look around the inner prison and the Lord Almighty would be there. Even in the darkness of the dungeon the Lord is with and keeps them. Paul and Silas knew in their hearts that even though their feet were in the stocks, the Lord was right there next to them. Paul and Silas were not concerned with their situation or the harsh treatment they received. Even in the darkness of the dungeon they saw the living Lord God Almighty's light. *It is all a mind thing!*

Like Paul and Silas – *It is all a mind thing!* We should focus our mind and attitude on the living and true God. We must realize the Lord Almighty is saying *"I will never leave you, I will never abandon you, I will never leave you alone, I will never leave you in this place of hurt, and I will never leave you when you are troubled and distressed, I will keep you and I will strengthen you."* We must make up our mind and set our thoughts on the Lord and pray and sing a *Prayer of Protection* as Paul and Silas did. *It is all a mind thing!*

A Prayer of Dependency

    "He only is my rock and my salvation; He is my defense; I shall not be greatly moved" *(Psalm 62:2).*

"My soul, wait thou only upon God; for my expectation is from Him" (Psalm 62:5).

Next, Paul and Silas prayed and sang a *"Prayer of Dependency."* Paul and Silas made up their mind that the Lord Almighty was their rock and defense. Their attitude was that the situation and harsh treatment would not greatly move nor shake them because they depended on the Lord as their rock and salvation. Paul and Silas' mindset was deeply and firmly rooted in the word of God. They depended on the Lord and knew in their mind and heart that the Lord was on their side. Paul and Silas' mind, heart, attitude and spirit screamed dependency on the Lord. Their soul waited only upon God because their expectation was from Him. Paul and Silas were beaten and in shackles, but nevertheless they expected deliverance, protection and liberty from the Lord. We should be like Paul and Silas, not caring what is happening around and to us because our soul waits only for the Lord Almighty. *It is all a mind thing!*

Everyone that labors and is heavy laden can come unto the Lord and find rest for his soul. This should be our mindset. Our situations, trials and burdens cannot hold us because, like Paul and Silas, our expectation is from the Lord Almighty! *It is all a mind thing!*

Our mind should expect the anointing to destroy our yokes. Our mind should expect where the Spirit of the Lord is there is liberty. Our mind should expect healing. Our mind should expect deliverance. Our mind should expect the Lord to bring us to a place of safety. Our mind should expect the Lord to keep us. *It is all a mind thing!*

Paul and Silas prayed and sang a *"Prayer of Dependency"* because they knew they served a God who loved them. They knew that the Lord Almighty was in the darkness of the dungeon and He was along with and was standing next to them. They also were able to pray and sing a *"Prayer of Dependency"* because their mind and attitude told them that all things work together for good to them that love God, to them who are the called according to His purpose. *It is all a mind thing!*

A Prayer of Trust

"The LORD is my shepherd; I shall not want. He maketh me to lie down in green pastures: He leadeth me beside the still waters. He restoreth my soul: He leadeth me in the paths of righteousness for His name's sake. Yea, though I walk through the valley of the shadow of death, I will fear no evil: for thou

art with me; thy rod and thy staff they comfort me" (Psalm 23:1-4).

Third, Paul and Silas prayed and sang a *"Prayer of Trust."* Have you ever thought about Psalm 23? Because the Lord is our shepherd we do not have to worry about anything because we have the Lord who will lead, guide and direct us. The Lord as our shepherd will guide us into a safe place. He will ensure that wherever we go and wherever He takes us will be a place of safety and protection. The Lord as our shepherd means that we shall not want, or in other words, we should not lack anything. The Lord will take care of all our needs and concerns. *It is all a mind thing!*

Yea, though we walk through the valley of the shadow of death, we will not fear evil because the Lord is with us and His rod (power) and staff (authority) will comfort us. Paul and Silas' minds reflected upon this, which is why they prayed and sang a *"Prayer of Trust."* Paul and Silas' harsh treatment and imprisonment in the darkness of the dungeon was their valley of the shadow of death. We must understand the valley of the shadow of death is a place of darkness and loneliness, a place where problems and tribulations bound us and in this valley our situations will grab hold of us and not want to let us go. *It is all a mind thing!*

The valley of the shadow of death is where the thief comes not, but for to steal, to kill and to destroy us. What Paul and Silas knew in their minds and what our minds need to grab hold of was that yea, though we walk through the valley of the shadow of death we do not have to fear because the Lord is there with us. His power and authority will comfort us throughout the valley of the shadow of death. Our mind and attitude must know the Lord Almighty's power can deliver us and the authority of His word can set the captives free. That is why Paul and Silas prayed and sang a *"Prayer of Trust." It is all a mind thing!*

Paul and Silas were not concerned about being in the valley of the shadow of death. Likewise, we should not be concerned when we find ourselves in that same valley, nor should we fear our problems, trails, situations, circumstances and tribulations. We should not sit down before the Almighty and pitifully cry out woe is me because I lost my job, woe is me because I cannot pay the rent or mortgage and woe is me because I am sick and alone. When reproach has broken our heart and we are full of heaviness, we should not look in the valley of shadow of death for someone to pity and comfort us. *It is all a mind thing!*

It is our chronic inclination to look for fulfillment in all the wrong places. We often look for pity and comfort in others while tending to believe that the Almighty is not enough. That is when we rely on our own self-sufficiency – the stubborn independence that makes us deal with our problems and concerns in our own way apart from our Lord Jesus Christ. Unfortunately, this causes us to focus on and linger in the valley of the shadow of death. It is in this valley that most people eventually come to a place where God is all that they have and discover that God is all they need. *It is all a mind thing!*

It is at this time they come to know God Almighty as El Shaddai – the God who is more than enough; more than sufficient. In the midst of pain, El Shaddai says "I am more than enough." When faced with problems we may fret, but El Shaddai says "I am more than enough." When reproach has broken our heart and we are full of heaviness, El Shaddai says "I am more than enough." Financial difficulties may try to drag us deeper into the darkness of the valley of the shadow of death, but El Shaddai says, "I am more than enough." In the valley of the shadow of death, we should rightfully and gleefully turn our hearts towards God Almighty. It is God who will meet our needs because He is El Shaddai – the God who is more than enough; more than sufficient. El Shaddai is more than enough to meet our eternal needs. El Shaddai is more than enough to meet our spiritual needs. El Shaddai is more than enough to meet our emotional needs. El Shaddi is more than enough to meet our directional needs. El Shaddi is more than enough to meet our physical needs. *It is all a mind thing!"*

We should be like Paul and Silas and pray and sing a *"Prayer of Trust,"* then righteously expect the Lord's salvation and defense to set us up on high. In the valley of the shadow of death our mind and attitude should be such that we will praise the name of God with a song and will magnify Him with thanksgiving. This indeed will please the Lord! *It is all a mind thing!*

In the valley of the shadow of death our mind and attitude should be of one accord, causing our heart to sing out that we serve a mighty God. In the midst of the valley of the shadow of death, our attitude should loudly declare that we serve a God that loves, cares about us and can deliver us. Yea, though we walk through the valley of the shadow of death, we will not fear evil because the Lord has not given us the spirit of fear, but of power and of love and of a sound mind. While in the valley we should stir up our mind by remembering it is the Lord Almighty that comes so that we might have life and have it more abundantly. *It is all a mind thing!*

We should lift up our heads in the valley of the shadow of death and the King of Glory shall come in. Who is this King of Glory? The LORD strong and mighty, the LORD mighty in battle. So when we find ourselves in a situation, in trouble, in turmoil, in distress and deep in the mire and muck, just remember lift up your head and the King of Glory shall come in. Paul and Silas knew this and that is why the inner prison and the darkness of the dungeon could not keep them in the valley of the shadow of death. That is why Paul and Silas prayed and sang a *"Prayer of Trust." It is all a mind thing!*

While we must get it in our minds that the valley of the shadow of death does exist, more importantly, we must understand, without wavering in our minds, that whoever dwells in the secret place of the most High shall abide under the shadow of the Almighty. We have to realize that being under the shadow of the Almighty counters the power of the valley of the shadow of death. Darkness, trouble and pitfalls run rampant in the valley of the shadow of death, but under the shadow of the Almighty, we find the Lord Jesus Christ in all His glory and in Him is life and that life is the light of men which shines in darkness.

Refuge, fortress and trust await those who abide under the shadow of the Almighty. *It is all a mind thing!*

We can be deep in the mud, stuck in the mire and up to our waist in trouble, but if we remember in our mind that we dwell in the secret place of the most High, we shall abide under the shadow of the Almighty. Being under the shadow of the Almighty means that God will step in and cast His shadow over us and his protection is underneath it. Under that shadow is His love, under that shadow is His caring and compassion and we can walk under it. Under the shadow of the Almighty we do not have to be concerned about the valley of the shadow of death because the Lord is our strength and we have a refuge and in Him we can trust. *It is all a mind thing!*

So what Paul and Silas did and what we should also do when we find ourselves in a situation and trouble, is remember that God is our strength and refuge. What does it mean when it says that God is our refuge? Simply put, it means that we can step into God and settle into God and His comfort. Under the shadow of the Almighty we can abide in the rest and peace of the Almighty. In this refuge of protection under the shadow of the Almighty, trust exits where we can trust in Him and hold onto His love. *It is all a mind thing!*

While in the valley of the shadow of death we need to take refuge under the shadow of the Almighty and learn to implicitly trust God, the Almighty. We need to learn to trust our Lord Jesus Christ as the good shepherd because He alone knows the best way to guide and lead us through the perils and pitfalls in the valley of the shadow of death. *It is all a mind thing!*

The good shepherd not only knows the best way we should go, but those who rely on and trust Him will surely come through the valley of the shadow of death even though they may be troubled on every side, yet not distressed; perplexed, but not in despair; persecuted, but not forsaken; cast down, but not destroyed. Additionally, those who trust the good shepherd will emerge from the valley bearing about in their body the dying of the Lord Jesus that the life of Jesus might be made manifest in their body. Those who trust the good shepherd will ultimately find comfort and rest in the Lord Jesus Christ's strength, joy and peace. It is our responsibility to follow the good shepherd and remember all the ways the LORD thy God led you while in the valley of the shadow of death. *It is all a mind thing!*

A Prayer of Praise

> *"Make a joyful noise unto the LORD, all ye lands. Serve the Lord with gladness: come before His presence with singing"* *(Psalm 100:1-2).*

Paul and Silas prayed and sang a *"Prayer of Praise."* How was it possible for them to pray and sing a *"Prayer of Praise"* when they had been harshly treated, beaten and thrown into the inner prison? How could they pray and sing a *"Prayer of Praise"* when they were without food, in darkness and had their feet in stocks? Yet their mind and attitude compelled them to pray and sing a *"Prayer of Praise."* They purposed in their mind to make a joyful noise unto the Lord and come before His presence with signing. *It is all a mind thing!*

When we find ourselves in harm's way, in trouble and in difficulties, why does the scripture tells us to make a joyful noise and come before His presence with signing? *It is all a mind thing!* It is all an attitude; it is all the way we feel in our heart. When we bow before His presence and worship Him, our mind, attitude and heart are all saying "Lord Almighty we are magnifying and lifting you before our problems." Our mind should want to keep the Lord, the King of

Glory before our face. We should not look at our concerns and problems, but only look at the mighty God, the eternal Father, the Alpha and the Omega! Our mind should be so riveted to the Lord that the only plausible thing to do is to open our mouths to pray and sing a *"Prayer of Praise"* to the Lord. When we begin to pray to the Lord and sing praises to Him, our focus is then lifted up to the God that we serve. Our eyes stare in the face of God and see His strength and everything that God is, which causes us to overlook our being in bondage and our circumstances that are trying to keep us down. This is what was occurring in the mind of Paul and Silas. *It is all a mind thing!*

A Prayer of Promised Help

"I will lift up mine eyes unto the hills, from whence cometh my help (Psalm 121:1)

Fear thou not; for I am with thee: be not dismayed; for I am thy God: I will strengthen thee; yea, I will help thee; yea, I will uphold thee with the right hand of my righteousness. For I the LORD thy God will hold thy right hand, saying unto thee, Fear not; I will help thee" (Isaiah 41:10, 13).

"For David speaketh concerning Him, I foresaw the Lord always before my face, for He is on my right hand, that I should not be moved" (Acts 2:25).

Finally, Paul and Silas prayed and sang a *"Prayer of Promised Help."* Their mind, attitude and heart told them to fear not in their trouble and not to let strongholds pull them down. The Lord Almighty, just like He was to Paul and Silas, is with us and is a promised help in our time of trouble. The two of them were in the darkness of the dungeon with their feet shackled in the stocks, but their mind said fear not, for God will strengthen, help, uphold and hold thy right hand. When we are really in trouble, like Paul and Silas, our mind needs to remember not to be dismayed, for the Lord Almighty is our God and He will never leave nor forsake us. *It is all a mind thing!*

The Almighty will never abandon us because He is our God! We may be in a situation or circumstance, but the Lord will strengthen us and hold our right hand as He whispers into our ear *"fear not, I will help thee."* Our mind should focus on this promise of help as we realize the Almighty is holding our right hand. When we are in the midst of troubles, trials and tribulations, the Lord is there. He holds our right hand because that is the place of power. The right hand is where God manifests healing and deliverance. When God holds our right hand He is saying I am ready to release you unto deliverance. I am ready to destroy your yokes. I am ready to strengthen you. It is at this moment that our mind should tell us to grab His hand tightly and just squeeze it, keeping the Lord always before our face. *It is all a mind thing!*

When we keep the Lord before our face, we will see the Almighty everywhere we look. We are not looking at our problems and concerns but the face of the Almighty. Our mind should be overwhelmed with the thought and desire to seek the Lord's face, to look upon His strength with joy in our heart and to grab His right hand while thinking about the Lord Almighty's love. Situations, problems, circumstances, trials and tribulations should not move nor shake us. We have to get it in our mind that the Lord Almighty is on our right hand to securely hold and lift us up above obstacles, problems and trials. *It is all a mind thing!*

Paul and Silas made up their minds that they would still pray and sing *a "Prayer of Protection, a Prayer of Dependency, a Prayer of Trust, a Prayer of Praise and a Prayer of Promised Help,"* regardless of what came their way. As a result of their mindset and a God-focused attitude, the perfect will of God manifested itself in the inner prison. At midnight, as Paul and Silas prayed and sang these prayers of praise unto God, the prisoners heard them. Just imagine the thoughts that went through the prisoners' minds as they heard Paul and Silas joyfully pray and sing these prayers of praise unto God. It is probably safe to assume their focus shifted from their own imprisonment and being cast into the darkness of the dungeon to the peace of God, which passes all understanding. Additionally, these prayers of praise unto God kept the prisoners' hearts and minds through Christ Jesus. Then suddenly these prayers of praise caused a great earthquake to shake the foundations of the prison and immediately all the doors were opened and everyone's bands were loosed. Paul and Silas' mindset, God-focused attitude and prayers of praise delivered the captives and broke the chains. *It is all a mind thing!*

Paul and Silas had the right mindset and God-focused attitude and as a result of their prayers of praise unto God, He immediately opened all the doors and set everyone free. At this moment in eternity, the Lord's perfect will was accomplished not only in the prison but in the keeper of the prison and his house-hold as well. Paul and Silas' mindset, God-focused attitude and prayers of praise persuaded the keeper

of the prison to ask "what must I do to be saved?"
Subsequently, Paul and Silas told the keeper of the
prison to believe on the Lord Jesus Christ and thou
shalt be saved and thy house. *It is all a mind thing!*

I DO WHAT THE WORD SAYS I CAN DO

Reality Two

"Verify, verify, I say unto you, He that believeth on Me, the works that I do shall he do also; and greater works than these shall he do; because I go unto my Father" (John 14:12).

As Believers, we need to embrace the very words Jesus Christ spoke when He said that we shall not only do the works He did but greater works than He. Failing to do what the word says leads to big problems in the Body of Christ today. Most Believers will quickly agree that they believe what the word of God says, yet oftentimes we do not do what the word says we can do.

We tend not to walk in what the word tells us we can do, instead wanting to walk in what our flesh is saying and in how we feel or "I feel good *fleshly* syndrome." As Believers, we must come to a place in God where we become "doers" of His word and realize that when we believe on Jesus Christ, we can do the works that Christ did and even greater works than Jesus Christ. When we do what the word says we can do, we will receive whatsoever things we say shall come to pass and nothing shall be impossible for us.

Once we know God's will, we should adjust our lives to Him and His purposes and destiny. God's desire is for us to become involved in what He is doing. Understanding what our Father is doing helps us to know what the Father wants to do through us for His kingdom and glory. Further, when we do what the word says we can do, it propels us in the center of where God wants us to be. It causes our Father to open His heart, reveal Himself and draw us into His secret place.

Chapter 10

I CAN DO THE WORKS
AND GREATER WORKS
THAN JESUS CHRIST DID

*"Verify, verify, I say unto you, He that believeth
on me, the works that I do shall he do also;
and greater works than these shall he do;
because I go unto my Father" (John 14:12).*

G od gave us an identity when He made us in His
image, likeness and to have dominion. Our God
and Father fearfully and wonderfully made us in His
image and likeness so that we can fulfill Reality Two–*I
can do what the word says I can do*. John 14:12 is an
excellent place to begin to understand Reality Two.

This passage of scripture is very thought-pro-
voking! Can you imagine as Believers we can do the
works that Christ did and even greater works than

Jesus Christ? Some in the Body of Christ may find this truth hard to believe, while others are skeptical, at best. As a result, signs and wonders follow them that believe while fleeing from those who disbelieve, because their unbelief causes them to habitually walk in their doubt and skepticism. Nevertheless, Jesus Christ clearly stated and revealed in the scripture a very powerful kingdom principle–that *we can do the works that Christ did and even greater works than Jesus Christ.*

Jesus Christ gave us a Helper, the Holy Spirit, to abide with us forever. The Holy Spirit helps us to become more and more like Jesus Christ to make the life of a Believer a mirror image of Jesus Christ. We cannot do these works that Jesus Christ did apart from the eternal Father who dwells in us. He does the works through His Spirit. That is why we have the Holy Spirit to guide us into all truth, for He shall not speak of Himself; but whatsoever He shall hear, that shall He speak and He will show us things to come. Subsequently, the eternal Father, according to the power that works in us, empowers us to do the very works that His only Begotten Son did. Therefore, let us examine the kingdom principle that Jesus Christ stated and revealed in John 14:12.

He That Believeth On Me

The very first thing to notice concerning doing the works that Jesus Christ did is we must believe on Jesus Christ as well as believe the works He did. As a matter of fact, in John 10:37, 38 Jesus tells us *"If I do not the works of my Father, believe me not. But, if I do, though ye believe not Me, believe the works: that ye may know and believe that the Father is in Me and I in Him."* Basically, what Jesus Christ is saying is believe what I do, believe the works, believe the miracles and believe that the eternal Father is in me and that I do what the Father does. It is extremely important for us to believe, because it is the key that releases the Holy Spirit's power and might exceedingly and abundantly in our lives and causes us to see the very glory of God.

The Works That I Do

Jesus Christ did not do His works apart from the eternal Father. Instead, Jesus Christ did the works which the Father gave Him to finish. Furthermore, the works Jesus Christ did bore witness of Him and that the eternal Father sent Him. The works of Jesus Christ are written that we might believe that Jesus is the Christ, the Son of God and that believing we might have life through His name. Some well-known works of Jesus Christ are:

- Turned the water into wine (John 2:1-11)
- Displayed power to heal all manner of sickness and disease among the people (Matthew 4:23-24)
- Cleansed the lepers (Matthew 8:1-3; Luke 17:11-19)
- Multiplied food to feed thousands (Matthew 14:19-21; Mark 8:1-9)
- Walked on water (Matthew 14:25)
- Cast out devils (Matthew 8:28-32)
- Calmed the storm and waves (Mark 4:37-39)
- Raised the dead (Mark 5:38-42; John 11:43-44)

Shall He do Also?

Look closely at the Great Commission and Jesus Christ's sending out of the twelve disciples, which contain the Believer's source of authority and power which is rooted in His name. Jesus Christ commissioned Believers, in His name, to cast out devils and to lay hands on the sick. When we believe on Jesus Christ and fully exercise this source of power, we will do the works of Jesus Christ which will ultimately bear witness about and point people to our Lord and Savior. But, in order to do this, our hearts must be in unity with God's heart! Our hearts must match God's will! Our hearts must align with the purposes of the Almighty!

God has to shape, mold and develop our hearts and characters so that our lives flow into the center of His will in unity with His heart and character. The unity of the Heart of God and our heart cause the work of our flesh to cease and the Heart of God to begin. The union of our hearts makes it possible for God to reveal Himself and for us to receive what is in the Heart of God.

This divine union transcends us beyond just hearing the voice of God and makes it possible for us to see what the Almighty is doing as well as what He plans to do. Subsequently, when our hearts are in unity and right with the Heart of God, we begin to bear all things, believe all things, hope all things, endure all things, trust all things and obediently do all things the eternal Father desires, such as the works that Jesus Christ did. We must understand that unbelief does not limit the power, the works that Jesus Christ did or the works that we shall do also. Unfortunately, unbelief keeps people from bringing their sick and diseased to be healed.

We do not readily see signs, wonders and miracles in the Body of Christ because the average Christian does not fully embrace the truth of God's word and step into the fullness of Jesus Christ. The Body of Christ has to embrace God's word, believe on Jesus Christ, step into Jesus Christ and exercise the authority and power He gives us. Jesus Christ commanded the twelve, *"And as you go, preach, saying, 'The kingdom of heaven is at hand.' Heal the sick, cleanse the lepers, raise the dead and cast out demons."*

Once this happens, the signs, wonders and miracles will follow. We must realize that God does not leave the confirmation of so great salvation to men alone, He also bears witness both with signs and wonders and with divers miracles and gifts of the Holy Ghost, according to His own will (Hebrews 2:3-4).

Greater Works Than These Shall He Do

God fearfully and wonderfully made and endowed us with power to do the works that Christ did and even greater works than Jesus Christ. Jesus Christ promised that *"the works that I do shall he do also; and greater works than these shall he do; because I go to my Father."* This promise doubtless had a special reference to the apostles themselves. But to limit the passage to only the apostles robs other Believers in the Body of Christ of the benefits of this promise. John 14:12 clearly states *"He that,"* a reference to each and every Believer! Do not make any mistake about it, anyone who believes on Jesus Christ can walk in this promise from the Lord. As a matter of fact, our Lord Jesus Christ is not saying we will do greater miracles than He did, but just as equally, and that our effect on people, our influence and our ministry will be greater, more extensive and more widespread, reaching all the nations.

Because I Go Unto My Father

Jesus Christ closes John 14:12 with "*Because I go unto my Father.*" As Jesus Christ went to the Father, we received the Promise of the Father which is the gift of the Holy Spirit. We receive God's power when the Holy Spirit comes upon us. We need this power to effectively serve the eternal Father, to boldly preach, to heal the sick, cleanse the lepers, raise the dead and cast out demons. Because of this, we should not attempt ministry without God's power because it is only through His power that we shall witness for Jesus Christ to the end of the earth, reaching all nations.

Chapter 11

I CAN DO NOTHING WITHOUT GOD

"I can of mine own self do nothing: as I hear, I judge: and my judgment is just; because I seek not mine own will, but the will of the Father which hath sent me" (John 5:30).

"Then said Jesus unto them, When ye have lifted up the Son of man, then shall ye know that I am He, and that I do nothing of myself; but as my Father hath taught me, I speak these things" (John 8:28).

Our Father fearfully and wonderfully made us so that we can do nothing without God, on our own accord or through our wisdom. This is why our eternal Father loves us and shows us all things that He does because our flesh limits our knowledge, wisdom and power. Therefore, we should be like Jesus Christ and do nothing on our own accord or authority, but instead say and do exactly what the eternal Father teaches us through His Holy Spirit. As born again Believers abiding in the Body of Christ, we must get it in our spirit and fully understand that it is the eternal Father who orders our steps concerning what to do, what to say and what to proclaim. We should not desire to seek our own counsel or will, or do those things we think are right in our own eyes, but only the will and pleasure of the eternal Father.

We are nothing, we can do nothing and have nothing good in us apart from the Lord. However, if we remain in the Lord and He in us, we will bear much fruit. Matthew 7:20 tells us that we shall be known by our fruits. In other word, the fruit that comes from the life of a disciple of Jesus Christ should bear witness of Jesus Christ's love and character.

The fruits refer not only to actions of our lives, but also to the doctrines we proclaim. The doctrines we proclaim should consistently produce fruit in our lives that bears evidence of a life that is of God and point people toward Jesus Christ as our Lord and Savior. As a matter of fact, Jesus Christ chose, ordained and commissioned us to go forth into the world and bring forth much fruit that remains.

In order to bear much fruit, we must abide in the Lord Jesus Christ. All that we are, do, or have must originate from our abiding in the Lord and He in us. We must have union with Him by faith. We must allow Him to cleanse and teach us by His word. We must remember and adhere to the fact that our Lord Jesus Christ is the true Vine and the Father is the husbandman. We must fully engage this spiritual truth in order to see the infinite wisdom, knowledge, resources and faithfulness of God, the Husbandman of His vineyard.

In essence, the eternal Father takes loving care of all the branches of the Vine, that is, all Believers who through obedience to the Gospel, who by faith are united to our Lord Jesus Christ. Consequently, we must accept that the Lord as the true Vine will repeatedly prune us to make us bear richer and more excellent fruit. It should also be a great concern among all Believers to bear much fruit because our fruitfulness under the tutelage and watchful eye of Jesus Christ proves that we are His true followers or disciples.

Even though we are nothing and can do nothing apart from the Lord, we can do all things through Christ which strengthens us. It is through Jesus Christ, His strength, and abiding in Him that we will know

His love, experience His power, walk in continual victory and witness much fruitfulness in our lives. It is this much fruitfulness that honors and glorifies the eternal Father.

Chapter 12

I DO WHAT I SEE MY FATHER DOES

"Then answered Jesus and said unto them, Verily, verily, I say unto you, The Son can do nothing of Himself, but what He seeth the Father do: for what things soever He doeth, these also does the Son likewise" (John 5:19).

To do what we see the eternal Father doing is rooted in the relationship our Lord Jesus Christ initiated and established. But most importantly, our level of fellowship and intimacy with our Lord nurtures and heightens our ability as well as our desires to do what we see the Father has done. Psalm 37:4 reminds us that when we delight ourselves in the Lord, He shall give us the desires of our heart. This means as we draw close to the Lord in fellowship and intimacy, allowing the Spirit of the living God to work in and through us, we will see our desires to do what the Father does manifested, ultimately glorifying God when we do what He does.

Our level of fellowship and intimacy positions us so that the Holy Spirit can diligently cultivate the desire within our hearts to do the deeds of the Father. The unity of the Heart of God and our heart cause the work of our flesh to cease and the Heart of God to begin. It is at this moment that we will start to see what the eternal Father is doing, over and above hearing His voice. The union of our hearts makes it possible for the Holy Spirit to reveal truths to us so we might see what the eternal Father is doing as well as what He plans to do. Subsequently, when our hearts are in unity and right with the Heart of God, we begin desiring to do all the things that we see the eternal Father does and what He will do.

In this season, as born again Believers abiding in the Body of Christ, we must constantly ask ourselves what is God doing and what does He plan to do? Unfortunately, many in the Body of Christ tend to focus a great deal of their effort only on what God has already done. While there is nothing wrong with remembering, praising, honoring and glorifying the eternal Father for what He has done, this tends to lock us into a mindset of where the Lord has been and not where He is going, what He is doing or what He plans to do! Regrettably, it causes us to only see the backside of the Lord and where His glory has already passed by. In order to advance the kingdom of God, we must be mindful of what God is both doing at the present and what He will do. It is only when we desire these two things that we will see the face of the Almighty.

When we constantly focus on what the Father has already done, not only are we limited to seeing the residual effects of God, if we continue in this mindset it will end up hindering our pursuit of the Almighty. This hindrance will sooner or later impede our maturity in the Lord. That is why we as the Body of Christ should not exclusively focus on what He has done and where the Father has already worked. We must remember that the eternal Father is always moving! If we recall during the journey in the wilderness, the Father told the nation of Israel that they had compassed Mount Seir long enough and it was time to turn and take their journey. Likewise He demands that we keep moving forward. We must continually turn to face the Lord and take our journey in order to move in cadence with Him. The only way we can move in sync with the Father is to position ourselves so that we can do what the eternal Father is doing and what He will do.

If we want the eternal Father to intimately speak with us, if we want to receive divine revelation and impartation from Him, we have to move forward in cadence with the eternal Father, do what He is doing and what He plans to do. It is when we move forward that we become conscious of what the eternal Father is doing and about to do. When we see and do what the Father is doing we become a reflection of the eternal Father.

We need to be attentive to the Holy Spirit's leading, guiding, teaching and prompting us so that we are better positioned to do only what we see the Father doing and what He plans to do. It is only then that we shall do all in the same way as the Father. At this point the question may arise, what is required for us to habitually do what the Lord does and will do? The eternal Father asks us to believe in the Lord whom He sent, that we cleave to, trust, rely on and have faith in the Father's Messenger. Then we will habitually do the works God does.

God is always at work and invites us to become involved in His work. This is why Jesus Christ declared *"My Father worketh hitherto, and I work" (John 5:17)*. We must understand, like Jesus Christ did, that the Almighty is already at work when He comes to us. God's desire is for us to move from where we are to where He is working and where He will work. God's invitation for us to become involved in His works means that we have to adjust our life to Him, His will, His purpose and His destiny. The precise moment God invites us is when we need to respond. Will we respond like Isaiah when he heard God's voice inviting him to become involved in His work? When God said, *"whom shall I send and who will go for us?"* Isaiah responded, *"Here am I, send me."* God revealed His work at the precise moment Isaiah accepted the invitation. God commanded Isaiah to go and preach to the people (Isaiah 6:8-9).

God begins to mold our character and heart to match His assignment when He invites us to join Him so that we are able to do what we see the Father does as well as what He will do. We must further understand that our Father has already begun working in us so that we may do His good works. The following verses illustrate this principle.

> *"For we are His workmanship, created in Christ Jesus unto good works, which God hath before ordained that we should walk in them" (Ephesians 2:10).*

"If a man therefore purge himself from these, he shall be a vessel unto honour, sanctified and meet for the master's use and prepared unto every good work" (2 Timothy 2:21).

"Make you perfect in every good work to do His will, working in you that which is well pleasing in His sight, through Jesus Christ; to whom be glory forever and ever. Amen" (Hebrews 13:21).

God fearfully and wonderfully made and designed us to do the same works as Him in perfect union with Him and His will. We should find comfort in knowing that God's unique design of us ultimately empowers us to do what He does, to fulfill His good works, His will, His purpose and His destiny. This helps us to understand, to realize and embrace our God-given identity so that we might glorify God to the fullest and do what we see the Father doing as well as what He will do.

Chapter 13

I SAY WHAT I HEAR MY FATHER SAYS

"For I have not spoken of myself; but the Father which sent Me, He gave Me a commandment, what I should say and what I should speak. And I know that His commandment is life everlasting; whatsoever I speak therefore, even as the Father said unto Me, so I speak" (John 12:49-50).

God the Father, God the Son and God the Holy Spirit are "speaking" beings. In Genesis we see how God the Father spoke everything into existence. God spoke the words *"let there be"* to nothing and nothing became something at the sound of His voice. When God speaks, His word does not come back void, but will accomplish the very purpose, that which pleases God and prosper in the thing whereby God sent the word (Isaiah 55:11).

Since God created us in His image and likeness, we too are "speaking" creatures. Therefore, it behooves us to learn and understand that the power of life and death are in the tongue. In other words, what we say either brings life or death. We should choose to speak a word of life so that both we and our seed may live by saying what we hear the Father saying. When we say what we hear the Father saying, we come into unity with God's will and begin to sound like the Father and tap into the Father's limitless power. Our voices change and sound like the voice of many waters and as the voice of a great thunder.

It is vitally important for us to become the voice of God in the earthly realm. Heaven, earth and the spirit realm hear our voices and cannot tell the difference between our voices once they begin to sound like the Almighty. Subsequently, when we say what we hear the Father says, in unity with the Father, sounding like the Father, the angels, that excel in strength, that do God's commandants, hearken unto the voice of the word and come for the word (Psalms 103:20). Amazing as it seems that the angels obey the voice of the word, even God, Himself, shows up when His word is proclaimed. Joshua 10:12-14 is an excellent example that illustrates this important God-ordained principle. When Joshua spoke, the sun stood still in the midst of heaven and the moon stayed for about a whole day. We further see that God hearkened unto the voice of a man because that voice came into unity with the Father's will and sounded like the voice of God, Himself.

When Satan and the enemy listen to the sounds coming from the face of the earth, they do not hear our sound but the voice of God. Regardless of how hard the enemy tries to listen and differentiate our voice from God's, the enemy cannot do so because our sound now distinctly sounds like the eternal Father and we have become the voice of God in the earthly realm.

Even though we come into unity with God's will, begin to sound like the Father and tap into the Father's limitless power, we have to learn to say what we hear the Father saying and speak the word. In this season of doing what we see the Father doing and saying what we hear Him saying, the Lord our God is rising up a group of people that shall listen to Him. A group of people that He can say *"I do not want to just speak to you. I want to reveal Myself to your inner man so that I may speak through you."* The eternal Father will put His words in our mouth and we shall speak all that the Father commands us to say.

We should let our speech at all times exude grace (gracious), inspiring trust, be pleasant and seasoned (as it were) with salt that we may know how we ought to answer every man. Furthermore, the Lord God will give us the tongue of the learned, that we should know how to speak a word in due season to those who are weary and heavy laden. This concept is vital for us to comprehend because the Lord's commandment means eternal life. This must be understood because it is the living Spirit of our holy God that quickens or gives life, whereas the flesh profits nothing. However, the words the eternal Father commands us to say are spirit and (eternal) life.

Just because we hear what God says does not mean we are to utter the word at the exact moment in eternity that we hear the Father. We must realize that not everyone is ready to hear and bear the word. We have to learn to wait for the unction, leading and guiding of the Holy Spirit before speaking what we hear the Father saying. Jesus Christ followed this principle when He told the disciples "*I have yet many things to say to you, but you cannot bear them now*" *(John 16:12)*. Further, Proverbs 15:23 proclaims that a word spoken in due season, at the right moment, is good, healthful and refreshing. When we have learned to say, in due season, what we hear the Father says, in

117

unity with the Father, sounding like the Father, then we should wait patiently on the Lord and let the Word do the work.

Chapter 14

I CAN STAND FIRM IN THE WORD

"Therefore, my beloved brethren, be ye steadfast, unmovable, always abounding in the work of the Lord, forasmuch as ye know that your labor is not in vain the Lord" (1 Corinthians 15:58).

God fearfully and wonderfully made us with the ability to grab His word, the tenacity to tightly embrace the word, the boldness to speak the word and the fierceness to stand firm in the word. Standing firm in the word makes us steadfast, unmovable and always abounding in the works of the Lord. Standing firm makes us immovable in spite of adversity. Standing firm in the word will keep us from being greatly moved because the Lord, the King of Glory, strong and mighty, mighty in battle is on our side and at our right hand (Psalms 16:8; 24:8; Acts 2:25).

Standing firm in the word releases our faith in God and nothing will shake that faith or move us away from the hope in Jesus Christ. Standing firm in the word produces faith that begins to hammer away at problems, situations, circumstances and adversities in our life. Standing firm in the word causes us to rise above our problems, situations, circumstances and adversities. Standing firm in the word causes us to take dominion and authority over these problems, situations, circumstances and adversities. Subsequently, boundaries, limitations and strongholds will not any longer have hold over our life when we rise above our problems, situations, circumstances and adversities in power, dominion and authority. When all this happens we will be able to declare the truth of Psalm 118:17 – "I shall not die, but live and declare the works of the Lord."

Standing firm in the word girths us with God's strength, power, might and makes our way perfect. Standing firm in the word gives us the power and the authority to speak boldly to problems, situations, circumstances and adversities, commanding them to move out of the way and they must move!

Standing firm in the word aligns us with the Father and His will as we realize that nothing is impossible for those who believe in Jesus Christ. Therefore, stand firm in the word because with God the possibilities are endless. The problems, situations, circumstances and adversities of our life not any longer have power to dictate our future, not when we align with God and stand firm in the word.

Affirmation

I shall not be greatly moved even in the face of distress. I shall stand firm in the word, not wavering and not taking my eyes off God, just standing firm in the word. I shall not be greatly moved despite being troubled on every side. I shall stand firm in the word, not bending, not giving up, just standing firm in the word. I shall not be greatly moved, even with trials trying to cast me down, not compromising my faith and my hope in God. I shall stand firm in the word!

Chapter 15

I CAN COMMAND AND RULE

"And God said, Let us make man in our image, after our likeness: and let them have dominion over the fish of the sea, and over the fowl of the air and over the cattle and over all the earth and over every creeping thing that creeps on the earth" (Genesis 1:26).

We know from John 1:3, Ephesians 3:9 and Colossians 1:16 that the eternal Father by Jesus Christ created all things that are in heaven and that are in earth, visible and invisible, whether they are thrones or dominions or principalities or powers, all things were created by Him and for Him. Jesus Christ, because He created all things, possesses the right of ownership overall and therefore rules over all. But, when God made man He entrusted His dominance over the earth to man.

Let Us Make Man In Our Image, After Our Likeness

Let us make man in our image, after our likeness, causes man to resemble God and qualifies man for dominion (the right and power to command, decide, rule, or judge) and constitutes man as the lord of all creatures. In creation, God equipped us with enough power to dominate and change anything to bring it into His divine order. Dominion is man's natural stewardship of the earth. Man's dominion extends from the fish of the sea to over all the earth to every creeping thing that creeps upon the earth to the moon and the stars.

In the Beginning God Gave Adam Authority

In the beginning, God gave Adam authority or the ability to rule over, dominate, enforce, modify, correct and govern everything within his sphere of influence. Unfortunately, Satan wanted the authority that God gave to man. Knowing that man could either use or misuse his God-given authority, he deceived Eve and caused Adam to sin. At that moment in time, Satan usurped man's authority. Just as God transferred some of His authority to man, man passed it on to Satan. But, Satan can only use his authority through man and can only influence the world to the degree that man chooses to sin.

Fortunately for us, our eternal Father had a plan. Herein is a great biblical truth – our faith is the victory because through faith Believers can stand fast and depend upon the victory our Lord Jesus Christ won when He overcame the world (John 16:33). Satan, the devil, is a defeated foe because our Savior defeated him, destroyed his works, spoiled his power, overcame and triumphed over him. Subsequently, the Body of Christ, through Jesus Christ's victory, regained the authority that Adam lost.

Our God-given authority through Jesus Christ makes it possible for us to dominate, rule, to govern and command. The eternal Father, through Jesus Christ, gives us authority not to charge out on a personal vendetta, hunting down the devil to engage him in combat, but to responsibly use our authority. Jesus Christ, Himself, provided the Body of Christ a lesson on retaliation.

"And when His disciples James and John saw this, they said, Lord, wilt thou that we command fire to come down from heaven and consume them, even as Elias did? But, He turned and rebuked them and said, Ye know not what manner of spirit ye are of. For the Son of man is not come to destroy men's lives,

but to save them. And they went to another village" (Luke 9:54-56).

The disciples were eager to command fire to come down from heaven because they did not yet fully understand the true mission of Jesus Christ. Christianity is not to be propagated by the sword because the Christian spirit is not one of retaliation.

We must learn this same retaliation lesson Jesus Christ provided to His disciples. Believers must always exercise self-control and act in knowledge, or else the very works we seek to help with will be destroyed. The lesson Jesus Christ wants each Believer to learn is that authority comes with the responsibility to use it for God's purpose and in the manner God intended for us to use it. The eternal Father wants us positioned so that we may readily assume power and authority in the spirit realm to rule and govern what happens in our sphere of influence. Then when people see us standing firm in the word of God, ruling, governing and commanding according to the eternal Father's will, they begin to see the kingdom and will of God validated in the earthly realm through us. This is why it is extremely important for us to realize spiritual authority is not an independent authority, but depends on our Lord Jesus Christ and us abiding in Him.

As we grasp the reality of Jesus Christ's retaliation lesson, we should be equally mindful when demonic powers challenge us in the course of going forth to teach all nations, baptizing them in the name of the Father and of the Son and of the Holy Ghost, when we deal with the demonic powers on the basis of our God-given authority in Jesus Christ. All Believers should get it in their hearts that our God-given authority gives us the right to rule over and dominate the devil and his fallen angels. We have the responsibility to rebuke the devil, take charge over his works and destroy them for the furtherance of the kingdom of God. Unless we rebuke the devil, he will not be rebuked and will not leave. It is time for the Body of Christ to realize that Satan, the adversary, is a *defeated foe* and rise up and take dominion over him.

But Satan, the defeated foe, holds some Believers in bondage. Our adversary binds the very ones who should be dominating him. Our adversary causes havoc when we should command him to go. Why is this possible? Why is this happening in the Body of Christ? Satan knows of our God-given authority and Jesus Christ's victory over him, but hopes we will remain ignorant of them. Unfortunately, our defeated altitude keeps us from walking a victorious life as more than a conqueror.

We are battle scarred but not victorious. We exercise some power but not authority. We survive but do not dominate that which we defeated. We have overcome but not as more than a conqueror. The Body of Christ seldom takes authority over the very things that it has defeated and conquered through its God given birthright as a child of the Almighty God. God wants us to exercise power and take authority and dominion, especially since Jesus Christ has already overcome the world. The Body of Christ simply has to embrace God's word, believe on Jesus Christ, trust in Jesus Christ, step into Jesus Christ and exercise the authority He gives us.

In the spiritual realm, if you do not believe you have authority, then you don't and you will not readily walk in and exercise your God-given authority. If our belief is weak, our expression of authority will also be weak and ineffective. Our eternal Father wants us to be bold and confident in the authority He releases to us through Jesus Christ to fulfill His purposes, to command and to govern in our sphere of influence.

Fellowship and intimacy are key and essential to authority. It is worthy to point out that our level of fellowship and intimacy with the Lord Jesus Christ result in our spiritual identity in Jesus Christ. Our measure of power and authority is uniquely tied to this spiritual identity in Jesus Christ. Our level of fellowship and intimacy with the Lord Jesus Christ is directly related to our authority in Him. Without close fellowship and intimacy, we do not have grounds for taking authority over Satan. Our fellowship and intimacy identify us in Christ and give us the privilege to command and rule. Our fellowship and intimacy hide us under the shadow of the Almighty. Our level of fellowship and intimacy and spiritual identity make it possible for Satan, when he looks at us to only see Jesus Christ, His power and His authority.

Satan and his demons know this. We must fully realize that the spirit realm recognizes and is familiar with the spiritual identity we exercise through our Lord Jesus Christ. Despite their power, they must submit and adhere to the authority we have been given. The seven sons of Sceva are a case in point.

These men knew of Paul and his fellowship, intimacy and spiritual identity in Jesus Christ, but they did not possess it themselves. Subsequently, they attempted to ride on Paul's coattails when they took it upon themselves to command those who had evil spirits and said *"We adjure you by Jesus whom Paul preacheth."* The evil spirit looked at the seven sons but did not see Jesus Christ, His power and His authority. That is why the evil spirit was able to say to them, *"Jesus I know and Paul I know; but who are ye?"* and the man in whom the evil spirit was leaped on them and overcame them and prevailed against them, so that they fled out of the house naked and wounded. (Acts 19:11-16).

In other words, the demonic spirit was saying he knew Jesus Christ beyond just an historical reference. He was saying, I know He is the Son of God, I know His power and His authority. Furthermore I know Paul, I know he is hidden in Jesus Christ and I know his spiritual identity is in Jesus Christ. I know He abides under the shadow of the Almighty and I know he exercises authority through Jesus Christ. When the demonic spirit looked at Paul, he did not see Paul but instead saw the face of the King of Glory, God the eternal Father, Jesus Christ, the Lord of Lords and Jesus Christ's power and authority steadfastly staring back at him. That is why our level of fellowship and intimacy and spiritual identity in Jesus Christ is vital to our ability to command and rule.

Chapter 16

I CAN COMMAND THE MOUNTAIN TO MOVE

"And Jesus said to them, Because of your unbelief: for truly I say to you, If you have faith as a grain of mustard seed, you shall say to this mountain, Remove hence to yonder place; and it shall remove; and nothing shall be impossible to you" (Matthew 17:20).

"Jesus answered and said unto them, Verily I say unto you, if ye have faith and doubt not, ye shall not only do this which is done to the fig tree, but also if ye shall say unto this mountain, Be thou removed and be thou cast into the sea; it shall be done and all things, whatsoever ye shall ask in prayer, believing, ye shall receive" (Matthew 21:21-22).

"For truly I say to you, That whoever shall say to this mountain, Be you removed, and be you cast into the sea; and shall not doubt in his heart, but shall believe that those things which he said shall come to pass; he shall have whatever he said " (Mark 11:23).

The essence of these scriptures is that God fearfully and wonderfully made us and gave us an identity in Him so we can boldly command mountains (barriers and hindrances) to move. Zechariah knew this all too well, as he recorded in the fourth chapter of the book named after him. Our eternal Father gave the prophet a vision to encourage Joshua and Zerubbabel to restore the temple and the nation of Judah.

The vision's purpose was twofold. First, for the prophet to remind Joshua and Zerubbabel that their true source of power was not by their might, strength or human power, but by the might and strength of the Holy Spirit. Second, to reassure them that despite the work on the temple being hindered and what seemed like an insurmountable task, Zerubbabel would finish the project. The lesson we need to learn is that despite the mountains we face in life, the Almighty God will strengthen us through His Holy Spirit, and as we begin to speak to the mountains, God, Himself assumes the responsibility to remove them.

When we exercise our God-given authority and dominion, we can righteously command mountains, which are barriers and hindrances such as diseases, finances, sicknesses, problems, tribulations and trials to move and they must obey! These mountains in our lives will load us down in an attempt to separate us from the word of God so that we might relinquish what the eternal Father has declared. Fortunately, our dominion over the mountains that attempt to hinder, obstruct, steal, destroy and kill us, invites God, the Almighty to rend the heavens and come down to check on us! When this happens, the mountains in our lives began to shake at the Father's presence.

As we continue to take power and exercise authority and dominion, God makes His name known to our adversaries, causing them to tremble at His presence. Further, we must remember that seemingly impossible situations that we face in our lives are actually divine opportunities to exercise and use our faith in a miracle-working God. It is during these seemingly impossible situations that we can stand firm in the word of God so that we can fulfill Reality Two—I *can do what the word says I can do*.

Oftentimes in our Christian walk with Jesus Christ we may sometimes continuously petition the Father to act on our behalf. But we need to know and clearly understand that the eternal Father calls us to establish His authority through our expressed action, belief in Him and by speaking His divinely empowered words of life. What we speak when united with faith is a very powerful moving and life changing force. When we trust, depend and lean on the Almighty God, He pours His Holy Spirit into our lives in fulfillment of the promise that He will never leave nor forsake us and the Holy Spirit strengthens us to face the mountains in our life. Consequently, when we have complete trust and faith in God and do not doubt in our hearts, we can boldly command the mountains of life to move.

Do not make any mistake about it, the mountains must obey. They must move, the mountains have to move, they will move and it is impossible for the mountains not only in our lives, but others as well, to continue to hinder, bind and obstruct the lives of God's people when we take power and exercise authority and dominion over them.

Chapter 17

I CAN TRUST IN THE WORD

"*Trust in Him at all times; ye people, pour out your heart before Him: God is a refuge for us. Selah*" (Psalms 62:8).

"*I will say of the LORD, He is my refuge and my fortress: my God; in Him will I trust*" (Psalms 91:2).

God's plan is for us to completely trust in Him for all of our needs. Our God-given identity provokes us to trust the eternal Father with all our heart at all times and lean not on our own understanding. This trust is the essence of having faith in God. From a Christian perspective, the definition of trust means trusting God and no other things. However, we tend not to walk and trust in what the word of God tells us we can do. Instead we want to walk and trust in what our flesh is saying and in how we feel, or the "I feel good *fleshly* syndrome." If we so choose, we can do what the flesh tells us to do. We can even do what is pleasing in our own eyes, but it is only through the Lord Jesus Christ and by His Spirit of Liberty that we find the freedom to be what we are by the grace of God and to fulfill Reality Two—I *can do what the Word says I can do.*

What it all boils down to is our trust in the word. Psalms 62:8 demands that we trust in the Lord at all times. We are to trust in the Lord regardless of what occurs in our lives. When we need love, trust in the Lord. When we are in doubt, put your trust in the Lord. When we are fearful, then trust in the Lord. When we do not understand, trust in the Lord. When we are sad, believe and trust in the Lord. When we desire God's abiding presence, then trust in the Lord. Trusting in the Lord and His word will keep us from being afraid of what the flesh can do unto us and causes:

- Our hearts to fix on the Almighty, His will, His purpose and His destiny for the Body of Christ
- Our spiritual eyes to see beyond heartaches, limitations and circumstances and to step into our God ordained purpose

- Us to lean not to our own understanding, but in all our ways to acknowledge the Lord (Proverbs 3:5-6)
- God to know us and for intimacy to flourish (Nahum 1:7)
- Our soul to become anchored, sure and steadfast in the word of the Lord (Hebrews 6:19)

When we truly trust in the Lord, our soul waits only upon God because our expectation is from Him. Not only will our soul wait upon God, we will tend to discover that trusting in the Lord causes us to readily obey, submit and surrender to the eternal Father's will and purpose. The more we trust in the eternal Father, the more He causes our spirit to see Him as our rock, our defense and see God as a refuge for us and our fortress.

Deep within our spirit the trust that we have for the eternal Father makes us immovable with a steadfast surety of victory in the face of adversity, tribulation, distress and persecution totally depend on Him. Additionally, trust causes us to confide and become secure in the Lord, forsaking all fear and trepidation that obstacles, trails, tribulations and problems may cause.

Trusting in the word reveals the truth of the word, which sets us free and keeps us from being tossed to and fro, wavering with every changing wind of doctrine, preventing us from falling prey to the cunning and cleverness of unscrupulous men utilizing every shifting form of trickery to mislead and deceive. Further, trust causes us to continually acknowledge the eternal Father in all our ways and stay in close fellowship and intimacy with Him. We will also begin to realize that the eternal Father fearfully and wonderfully made us so that we would completely trust Him and that trust nourishes our heart and fills our spirit.

We need to have enough confidence and trust in the word and the eternal Father that we will trust God with our most prized possessions, the very things that hold the greatest value to us. Once we are able to do this, we discover that we are blessed and surrounded by mercy because we have put our trust in the Lord.

Chapter 18

LET THE WORD DO THE WORK

"For the word of God is quick and powerful and sharper than any two-edged sword, piercing even to the dividing asunder of soul and spirit and of the joints and marrow and is a discerner of the thoughts and intents of the heart" (Hebrews 4:12).

God fearfully and wonderfully made and gives us His word to walk in and do what the word says. This is our God-given identity. His word is meant to order our steps and give us life. But, oftentimes because the word may seem strange and unusual to us, we do not put it on and walk in it. But, what if there is a place where we could go where the eternal Father could speak directly to us about our situation and a word is tailor made to fit our situation?

What if there is a place we could go where the Lord will tell us what to do, exactly when to do it and how to do it? In order to receive our deliverance, receive our healing and whatever we require of the Lord?

If there is a place like that would you go? Not only would you go, but would you be willing to go with both ears open, ready to hear what the Spirit of the Lord has to say? Would you go and obey the word, willingly submitting to its dictates? Would you go and surrender entirely to the word and be willing to let the word do the work? Or will you do what is recorded in the scriptures?

"Making the word of God of none effect through your tradition, which ye have delivered: and many such like things do ye" (Mark 7:13).

We know God's word is true and powerful. Isaiah 55:11 tells us that the word of God goes out and does not return void, but will accomplish and achieve the very purpose for which the eternal Father sends it. The word prospers in the very thing that God sent it forth to accomplish. But, how can God's word become of none effect? Do not these two verses appear to contradict each other? We know God's word does not change and is perfect, so how do we reconcile these verses? Mark 7:13 tells us when we have our own beliefs and traditions, when we expect the word to come a certain way, when we expect the word to cause our flesh to feel a certain way, when we expect it to look a certain way, then we make the word of God of none effect.

The word is still powerful and active. The word is still living, but if we do not submit to it, letting the word do its work, instead clinging to our situations and leaning toward tradition, while holding tight to our trials and tribulations, when we hold tightly to dead and dying situations, we make the word of none effect in our lives. However, when we submit to the word and are willing to obey it and let the word do the work, the very things we face in life are already dead through the power and glory of God's word. For example, David desired to defend his people and most importantly, God's name. Because David was confident and secure in the word of God, he did not focus on the person of Goliath or the physical situation around him.

David remembered and kept the Lord always before his face, knowing in his heart that the eternal Father was on his right hand and the Almighty would strengthen and help him. You see how David's faith in the word caused him to obey, submit and surrender to the word's power and he let it do the work. Oftentimes, we tend to look for something dramatic; however, the eternal Father looks for our humble obedience. Subsequently, our obedience and submission to the word, regardless of how strange the word may seem, manifests the power of the word. We just have to walk in the word and let it do the work.

Let us focus on and look closely at three specific examples recorded in the Bible where the word did the work.

- Jesus Heals a Deaf and Dumb Man

"And they bring unto Him one that was deaf and had an impediment in his speech; and they beseech Him to put His hand upon him. And He took him aside from the multitude and put His fingers into his ears and He spit and touched his tongue. And looking up to heaven, He sighed, and saith unto Him, Ephphatha, that is, Be opened. And straightway his ears were opened, and the string of his tongue was loosed and he spake plain" (Mark 7:32-35).

- Jesus Heals a Blind Man at Bethsaida

"And He took the blind man by the hand and led him out of the town and when He had spit on his eyes and put His hands upon him, He

asked him if he saw ought. And he looked up and said, I see men as trees, walking. After that He put His hands again upon his eyes and made him look up and he was restored and saw every man clearly" (Mark 8: 23-25).

- A Man Born Blind

"When He had thus spoken, He spat on the ground and made clay of the spittle and He anointed the eyes of the blind man with the clay. And said unto him, Go, wash in the pool of Siloam, (which is by interpretation, Sent.) He went his way therefore and washed and came seeing" (John 9:6-7).

First, Jesus heals a deaf and dumb man by putting His fingers into the man's ears, spitting and touching the man's tongue. In the next case, Jesus heals a blind man at Bethsaida by spitting on his eyes. Lastly, Jesus heals a man who was born blind when He spat on the ground and made clay from His spittle and used it to anoint the eyes of the blind man. Now let us return our focus to Mark 7:13 to understand how our tradition can make the word of none effect.

What would you do if someone spit on their hand and put it on your tongue, or spit on your eyes or put clay made of spit on your eyes? Right away we probably would say that is nasty, it is disgusting and gross. You are not going to touch my tongue, what is wrong with you?

How dare you to think that you can spit on your fingers and touch my tongue or spit in my eyes. You are not going to spit on me, or put that mud mixed with spit on my eyes.

What we need to realize is that this spit was anointed to heal. Regardless of what we think, how we feel or how strange it looks to us, in each of these cases this spit was anointed with healing power. Two people received their sight and another gained his speech. These three individuals did not hold on to their traditions nor allow them to tell them what it would take and what it would look like to experience the power of Jesus Christ, but instead they believed the very word of God and allowed it to do its work. Further, the three individuals abandoned traditions by taking a step of faith in the word, and their act of faith caused them to experience the power of the Lord Jesus Christ. The three individuals' obedience, submission and surrender to the word, regardless of how strange it seemed to them, manifested the power of the word.

How many of us will allow the word to do the work in our lives rather than holding on to tradition or the situations that bind us? Why? Because that situation has become comfortable and familiar, the pain has become bearable and we choose to tolerate the pain rather than step out into the unknown. But, we need to realize that the word of God is living and powerful. The word of God is sharper than a two edged sword, piercing even to the dividing asunder of soul and spirit and of the joints and marrow and is a discerner of the thoughts and intents of the heart.

When we rely on and let the word do its work, it will guide us and cut a pathway of safety through the unknown. The word will make the unknown become known. The word will pierce through every situation, every trail, every obstacle and every problem. We must get it in our spirit and heart that everything must align with and give way to the truth of the word. Not only shall we know the truth, but the truth will make us free and drive us directly into the peace, joy, comfort and rest of our Lord and Savior.

All we have to do is hold onto the word and step into those situations, into that trial and into troubles not with fear and trembling, but in power, authority and dominion. This is what the scripture means when it says we are more than a conqueror. We step in declaring healing, we step in announcing deliverance, we step in commanding the mountains and obstacles to get out of our lives, and we step in letting the word do the work. We dictate what the outcome will be. We have to get into our spirit and heart that the word gives us the power, authority and dominion to boldly call those things which are not as though they were.

Exercising dominance over the situation through the word of God allows us to fulfill Reality Two – I *can do what the word says I can do!* If you need healing, then declare healing because by the stripes of Jesus Christ we are healed. The mistake we make is that our body is aching, our body is sick and most people identify with their body. But realize we are a spirit. We possess a body, but we are a spirit. So we should not talk to our bodies but speak in the spirit realm, claiming what the eternal Father already has in store for us and taking dominion over the situation.

Do you realize that when we speak we set things in motion? Our words control our believing, our thinking, our behavior and even the direction our lives will take. The words we speak either bind or lose those ministering spirits mentioned in Hebrews 1:14. These ministering angels hearken to the voice of God's word. Hearken in Hebrew means "obey." Subsequently, the angels hear, come for and obey the words we speak in agreement with the Holy Spirit. We put the voice to God's words by speaking the word of God in the earthen realm in power, authority and dominion.

When we put all this together and begin to claim God's word, we actually come into agreement with what God has already said. We come into agreement with the Holy Spirit who searches the deep things of God and makes unction for us here on earth. The Holy Spirit already knows the heart and mind of God. Matthew 18:19 tells us why it is extremely important to come into agreement with the Holy Spirit.

"Again I say unto you, That if two of you shall agree on earth as touching anything that they shall ask, it shall be done for them of my Father which is in heaven" (Matthew 18:19).

When we claim and proclaim God's word, it gets His attention. Our proclamation of God's words inundate His ears with a thundering sound that the Lord meant to rise up from the face of the earth. When God hears His very own words rising from the earth He gravitates toward them. His word is already settled in heaven. So the eternal Father and the whole host of heaven are waiting to hear God's word and the truth rising up from the face of the earth spoken by us with power, authority and dominion.

Watch what happens! We here on earth, trust what we see and hear from the Holy Spirit. We lock arms with the Holy Spirit, begin to walk in lock-step with the Holy Spirit, proclaim the word in unity with the Holy Spirit and agree with the Holy Spirit. When we do these things, then anything we ask for in agreement with the Holy Spirit here on earth will be done by the eternal Father in heaven. At this point it behooves us to be very mindful of what is occurring in the spirit realm.

Our agreement and alliance with the Holy Spirit opens the windows of heaven connecting earth to heaven, the whole host of heaven and all that the eternal Father is. In this moment in eternity, truth springs out of the earth and righteousness looks down from heaven. As the words and truth spring up from the earth and meet righteousness in the atmosphere, an explosion takes place and manifestation happens! In the spirit realm a ladder is set up on the earth and its top reaches to heaven and we behold the angels of God ascending and descending on it to minister to those who shall be heirs of salvation.

These ministering angels help us to experience the fullness of the eternal Father's blessing and the richness of the destiny the Father has planned for each of us. At this time, if we listen closely and attune our hearts to the eternal Father and draw close to Him, we will hear the eternal Father say *"fear thou not; for I am with thee, be not dismayed; for I am thy God: I will strengthen thee; yea, I will help thee; yea, I will uphold thee with the right hand of my righteousness. For I the LORD thy God will hold thy right hand, saying unto thee, fear not; I will help thee."*

Our trials, tribulations, obstacles and problems may have us bent over and feeling like the prophet Jeremiah, when he said *"woe is me for my hurt! My wound is grievous."* When we grab ahold of God's word and the truth of His word, letting it do the work and start walking in the word, we will quickly realize that in that word is deliverance, in that word is healing, in that word is power, so as we walk our steps straighten up and we are not bent over any longer.

Our steps become sure because we realize with each step there is power in the word. There is love in the word, there is salvation in the word, there is peace in the word, there is joy in the word, there is happiness in the word, there is deliverance in the word, there is healing in the word, there is understanding in the word, there is hope in the word, and there is the eternal Father, the I AM THAT I AM, the Alpha and Omega, the beginning and the ending, resting in the very midst of His word. So let the word do the work that we shall fulfill Reality Two—I *can do what the Word says I can do!*

BY THE GRACE OF GOD I AM WHAT I AM

Reality Three

"But by the grace of God I am what I am and His grace which was bestowed upon me was not in vain" (1 Corinthians 15:10).

When Moses had a divine encounter with God, he asked, *"When I come unto the children of Israel and shall say unto them, The God of your Fathers hath sent me unto you and they shall say to me, What is His name? What shall I say unto them?"* God said unto Moses, *"I AM THAT I AM"* (Exodus 3:13-14). At this divine moment in eternity, God did not hesitate to reveal His identity to Moses. God was very clear and precise about His identity. As God was with Moses, He wants Believers to likewise be clear and precise about their identity. Our Father wants a

Believer to realize that by the grace of God, I am what I am. What God is saying is we need to fully embrace the fact that He fearfully and wonderfully made us, and by his grace we are what the word of God says that we are.

Chapter 19

I AM THE LIKENESS AND IMAGE OF GOD

"And God said, Let us make man in our image, after our likeness: and let them have dominion over the fish of the sea, and over the fowl of the air, and over the cattle, and over all the earth, and over every creeping thing that creeps on the earth" (Genesis 1:26).

God gave us an identity when He made us in His image, after His likeness and to have dominion over all the earth and every creeping thing on the earth. Our God and Father fearfully and wonderfully made us in His image and likeness so that we can embrace and fulfill Reality Three – *By the Grace of God I Am What I Am!*

Let us make man in our image, after our likeness causes man to resemble God, qualifies man for dominion (the right and power to command, decide, rule, or judge) and constitutes man as the lord of all creatures. Dominion is man's natural stewardship of the earth.

Let us make man in our image, after our likeness as an expression and revelation of the eternal Father's glory. We express, reveal and magnify God's glory as we walk through the valley of the shadow of death. This valley represents a place of darkness. It is a place where troubles, turmoil, confusion, trials and tribulations abound.

To stay in the valley of the shadow of death causes one's attention to focus entirely on trials, tribulations, situations and circumstances rather than the Lord. Distractions and troubles on every side will keep us in the valley of the shadow of death, causing us to stumble from trial to trial and facing tribulations in fear and without hope. However, when we focus on the Lord as our rock and draw close to Him, seek His face, depend and lean on Him and trust in Him, we can walk through this valley without fear and trembling because of the Lord's comfort and protection.

As we draw close to God, He draws close to us to reveal more of Himself and as we begin to dwell in the secret place of the Most High we shall abide under the shadow of the Almighty and not in the valley of the shadow of death. God wants us to know when we abide under the shadow of the Almighty we will never experience fear because the Lord is our light and salvation. We must realize that death is in the valley, whereas life abides under the shadow of the Almighty. It is when we abide under the shadow of the Almighty that we express, reveal, magnify and fill the earth with God's glory.

Furthermore, we express the eternal Father's glory when we are troubled on every side, persecuted, cast down, standing in the midst of trials and tribulations but staying rooted, grounded in, trusting, honoring and praising Him. It is at these moments that God receives glory and we fill the earth with the brightness of His glory. The earth beholds the glory of the Lord as we are changed into His image and likeness from glory to glory.

Satan, the adversary, would like us to stay in the valley of the shadow of death because in the valley, when a person loses hope darkness moves in and takes over, bringing with it despair, sadness and a lack of joy. The adversary tries to keep us in the valley and discourage us during times of trials and tribulations in order to prevent us from expressing and revealing God's glory.

We must fully understand that God created us in His image and likeness to express and reveal His glory and that Satan is not after us but the glory of God! Satan does not want the glory of God expressed and revealed. We must remember and hold fast to the fact that the sufferings of the present time are not worthy to compare with the glory which shall be revealed in us.

Let us make man in our image, after our likeness so that man can reflect who God is. At this moment in eternity, God is saying to the Body of Christ that man reflects who He is so there is someone that the earth can identify with who looks like us, loves like us, thinks like us, talks like us, lives like us and reflects power, authority and dominion like us.

Let us make man in our image, after our likeness means that we represent Him and act on His behalf in the earth. This is important to understand for two apparent reasons. First, our God and eternal Father fearfully and wonderfully made us in His image and likeness so that we can fulfill three realities – *to God be the glory, I can do what the word says I can do and by the grace of God I am what I am.* We are made in His image and likeness to represent all that God is, and at this moment in eternity, God looks into our eyes lovingly staring at Him and sees His own image reflected in miniature – that is what Psalm 17:8 means when it says "Keep me as the apple of the eye." Once we tap into His glory we can do what He does, say what He says, resemble and act like Him and reflect His glory. He made us in His image and likeness for His glory with the intended purpose for us to glorify and bless His glorious name and fill the whole earth with the knowledge of the glory of the LORD. As God made the angels to show forth His praise in the heavenly realm, God is saying to the Body of Christ, this day that we are in His image and likeness and created for Him that we should show forth His praise in the earthen realm. Secondly, Satan and the enemy cannot tell the difference between us and God because when we are beyond the veil we appear in the image of God, act like God and sound like God. Therefore, within the veil the only thing Satan can see and as far as Satan can see is all God and more of God.

Let us make man in our image, after our likeness because it is God's desire for us to live a life that glorifies and pleases Him and to use us as His witness in the earth to boldly profess that the Father is the "I AM THAT I AM" and proclaim with greatness, "oh LORD, our Lord, how excellent is Your name in all the earth!" Further, the Father created us in His image and likeness so that we will praise Him with our whole heart and declare the works of the LORD.

Let us make man in our image, after our likeness became a reality at the precise moment the LORD God formed man of the dust of the ground and breathed into his nostrils the breath of life and man became a living soul. This is paramount, because as a living soul created in the image and likeness of the Father, the Son and the Holy Spirit, all the fullness of the Godhead dwells bodily within us so that we can stand fast, immovable and always abound in the word of God despite situations, circumstances, problems and obstacles we encounter in life.

Chapter 20

I AM A SON AND A CHILD OF GOD

"For as many as are led by the Spirit of God, they are the sons of God. For you have not received a spirit of bondage again to fear; but ye have received a spirit of adoption whereby we cry, Abba! Father. The Spirit itself beareth witness with our spirit, that we are the children of God" (Romans 8:14-16).

"For it became Him, for whom are all things, and by whom are all things, in bringing many sons to glory, to make the captain of their salvation perfect through sufferings" (Hebrews 2:10).

When we receive Jesus Christ as our Lord and Savior, He gives us the power to become the sons (whether male or female) of God. Huios is the

Greek word for son and it refers to a son of character, a son bearing and manifesting the characteristics of the father. A son of character is one who embraces and fulfills Reality Three – *By the Grace of God I am what I am*.

We have not received the spirit of bondage (slavery) in order to relapse again into fear and trepidation, but God has given us the Spirit of adoption and sonship. Adoption is God's way of making a repentant sinner a member of His family so that the person might share the same rights and privileges as one born into the family.

God, before the foundation of the world, predestinated us unto the adoption of children by Jesus Christ unto Himself (Ephesians 1:4-5). As adopted sons we are more than a conqueror and able to take dominion and break every yoke and bondage. That is why God fearfully and wonderfully made us in His image and likeness and gives us an identity through the Spirit of adoption to be a son and a child of God.

Chapter 21

I AM A JOINT HEIR

"And if children, then heirs; heirs of God and joint-heirs with Christ: if so be that we suffer with Him, that we may be also glorified together" (Romans 8:17).

This verse holds a key to our identity in Jesus Christ. God fearfully and wonderfully made us to be His children, heirs of God and joint-heirs with Christ. As joint heirs we can embrace and fulfill Reality Three – *By the Grace of God I Am What I Am.* In order to fully understand this identity we must closely examine Romans 8:17.

And if children. As previously witnessed, God adopts repentant sinners as children of His family who share the same rights and privileges as one born into the family.

***Then heirs*.** When God treats us as His adopted sons we become heirs and are able to obtain an inheritance. It is noteworthy to point out that our inheritance is not just any inheritance to which the heir receives as a consequence of the former possessor's death – our inheritance is God, Himself and we are God's inheritance.

Heirs of God. Heirs of God means when we sustain the relationship of sons of God that we share the inheritance. It is extremely important for us to understand that this inheritance is neither an earthly nor a heavenly portion, but God Himself, is our portion (Psalm 16:5). God is our exceedingly great reward and inheritance. God, the *"I AM WHO I AM"* is infinitely greater and more glorious than heaven itself. Anything less than God, Himself, is insufficient and an unsatisfactory inheritance for the sons of God. As heirs of God we share in all that God is – His love, grace, mercy, holiness, righteousness, wisdom, power, truth and faithfulness. Not only is God our inheritance but we are God's inheritance.

And joint heirs with Christ. Jesus Christ, the Son of God, is heir to all the glory, power and authority in heaven and in earth (Matthew 28:18). It is especially noteworthy to understand that even though we are joint heirs, we do not have an inheritance apart from

Jesus Christ. However, in Jesus Christ, as joint heirs we partake in the eternal glory and are able to enjoy the same rights and privileges and receive the full riches and glory of what Jesus Christ, Himself, inherited.

God, the Father of our Lord Jesus Christ has blessed us with all spiritual blessings in heavenly places in Christ, specifically the heavenly realm where God rules and reigns. Now what does this has to do with our inheritance? First, nine blessings are directly interrelated to the salvation we enjoy (Ephesians 1:3-14):

- God blessed us with all spiritual blessings in heavenly places in Christ
- God chose us in love before the foundation of the world
- We are predestinated for Jesus Christ
- God adopted us as children by Jesus Christ
- God made us accepted in the beloved
- We have redemption through Jesus Christ's blood
- We have forgiveness of our sins
- We have obtained an inheritance
- We are sealed with the Holy Spirit of promise

Second, the Holy Spirit's seal upon us lets us know that we belong to the heavenly family. The Holy

Spirit's seal represents the advance installment of our inheritance until the fullness of the Spirit is received in anticipation of full redemption. The Believers' inheritance consists of eternal life, the final redemption at resurrection, the riches of the glory of His inheritance and all that is included in the riches of His grace. The riches of the glory of His inheritance means that God regards us as His inheritance, even as He is our inheritance. The riches of His grace extends to us the privilege of being raised up and seated together in heavenly places in Christ Jesus and that in the ages to come God might show the exceeding riches of His grace in His kindness toward us through Christ Jesus.

Oftentimes, we fail to appreciate the riches of His grace that cause Believers to sit in heavenly places in Jesus Christ. It is time for the Church to understand this aspect of our inheritance. When God raised Jesus Christ from the dead, He sat Christ at His own right hand in the heavenly places. Subsequently, because we inherit what Jesus Christ inherited, we too sit in the heavenly places.

This means that Believers are not any longer strangers and foreigners, but fellow citizens with the saints and of the household of God. Even though Believers live on the earth, our citizenship is in heaven and we are governed by God's invisible power that works in us. As such, we must be mindful that we sit in the heavenly places and our conversation is in heaven.

Take particular note of that – *our conversation is in heaven!* If we get this concept in our spirit and in our heart, then when we speak we will use the same power of conversation that is going on in the heavenly places. Our conversation will then originate from the heavenly places to consume, overpower, defeat and conquer the forces of Satan, as well as the obstacles, problems, situations, circumstances, hurdles and other distressing things in our lives.

If so be that we suffer with Him. The Church as a whole admirably partakes in the sufferings and hurts of its congregational members. Believers readily come together in prayer and fellowship to comfort those in distresses, troubles and hurts, lifting up one another's burdens (2 Corinthians 1:3-6). However, the problem is we have become selfishly consumed by our own hurts and the hurts of other suffering Believers. Consequently, Believers are left with little or no time to think on Jesus Christ's sufferings, let alone suffering with Him. However, we are commanded to suffer with Jesus Christ, know the fellowship of and partake of His sufferings. This is the inheritance of suffering – suffering as joint heirs with Christ.

"And if children, then heirs; heirs of God and joint-heirs with Christ: if so be that we suffer with Him, that we may be also glorified together" (Romans 8:17).

"That I may know Him and the power of His resurrection and the fellowship of His sufferings, being made conformable unto His death" (Philippians 3:10).

'But rejoice inasmuch as ye are partakers of Christ's sufferings; that, when His glory shall be revealed, ye may be glad also with exceeding joy" (1 Peter 4:13).

Critical to our suffering with Jesus Christ, fellowshipping and partaking of His sufferings is for us to understand the sufferings of Jesus Christ. On the way to Jerusalem with the twelve disciples, Jesus Christ foretold how He must go to Jerusalem and suffer many things–namely the sufferings of His death and resurrection.

Jesus, the Christ, told the disciples His sufferings would involve His betrayal to the chief priests and scribes, his condemnation to death, deliverance to the Gentiles, being mocked by the people, spitefully entreated, spit upon, scourge and crucifixion, but encouraged them that on the third day He would rise again (Matthew 16:21; 20:17-19; Mark 10:32-34; Luke 18:31-33).

The beatings and scourging our Lord Jesus Christ suffered were for our healing. The crucifixion He endured was for our salvation. As a result, Believers identify with Jesus Christ in salvation and receive the blessings of what Christ suffered. Christ Jesus endured all these sufferings for His body's sake, which is His bride, the Church (Colossians 1:24). As part of our fellowshipping and partaking of Christ's sufferings, our heavenly Father calls all Believers to suffer for the Church and for truth, preaching the gospel in all fullness.

When the bible refers to the sufferings of Jesus Christ abounding in us, it refers to sufferings we encounter for Christ, not the physical sufferings Jesus Christ endured. The more Believers suffer for Jesus Christ, the more grace and comfort will abound in their lives by our Lord and Savior. Additionally, Paul points out that we have the sentence of death in ourselves and are to be conformed unto His death. This means that we as Believers must personally walk out Jesus Christ's death in our lives. Ideally, this should lead us to decrease and die daily to self (flesh) (John 3:30; 1 Corinthians 15:31, 2 Corinthians 1:5, 9).

We have to remember that a greater intimate union with God requires death, not physical death but a spiritual death. We must die to our will and self (flesh)! To accomplish this, we should constantly set aside our thoughts, emotions, desires and any self-centered ways that are contrary to Jesus Christ. When we do this, we will decrease and Jesus Christ will increase. In other words, as we mature in Jesus Christ, man's words begin to decrease, or what we think God is, and God's words increase or what God actually is. Then, as we decrease and Jesus Christ increases in our lives, we begin to look more like Jesus Christ, sound more like Jesus Christ, act more like Him, offer love as the Father loves and give hope as He gives hope.

Our mandate for walking out Jesus Christ's death in our lives is Philippians 3:10. We can truly know Him and the power of His resurrection through the fellowship of His sufferings and be made conformable unto His death. The word of God informs us that death must precede "life."

"Verily, verily, I say unto you, Except a corn of wheat fall into the ground and die, it abideth

*alone: but if it dies, it bringeth forth much
fruit" (John 12:24).*

In order for our Father to fill us with all the fullness of the Godhead bodily, God has to first strip us
of our old self and self-centered ways that are not
pleasing to Him. As He does, we will decrease and
Jesus Christ will increase.

The increasing of Jesus Christ in our lives means
that Believers are always delivered unto death for
Jesus Christ's sake, that the life of Jesus might be
made manifest in our mortal flesh. Then the life of
Jesus Christ will be manifest in our mortal flesh
through the success of our ministry, the working
of miracles and the greater works that we shall do
because the Father has set Jesus Christ at His own
right hand in the heavenly places so that Believers
can give the fullest demonstration that Jesus Christ
rose from the dead. All of this causes us to conform
more into the image of His only begotten Son, and
subsequently God reproduces His exceedingly abundant Life in us. In essence, conformity to His image
is the result of our conforming to Jesus Christ's death.
This is the root meaning of Philippians 3:10.

Now that we have an understanding of the sufferings of Jesus Christ, we can truly know Him and the

power of His resurrection through the fellowship of His sufferings.

- First, the fellowship of His sufferings trans-forms our character and heart. Paul was well aware of this when he was inspired to write the last part of Philippians 3:10 (*the fellowship of His sufferings, being made conformable unto His death*). What Paul says here is that "I want to know the fellowship of His sufferings, I need to be conformed, molded, shaped and transformed into the likeness of Jesus Christ, even unto His death."

- Second, the fellowship of His sufferings pro-duces a certain level of commitment, intimacy and habitation with God.

- Third, the fellowship of His sufferings causes us to know the Father of our Lord Jesus Christ, the Father of mercies and the God of all com-fort. Who comforts us in all our tribulations, that we may be able to comfort them which are in any trouble, by the comfort with which we ourselves are comforted of God.

- Fourth, the fellowship of His sufferings gives us the tongue of the learned, that we should know how to speak a word in season to him that is weary and wakens our ear to hear as the learned.

- Fifth, the fellowship of His sufferings advances the kingdom of God and builds our confidence in Jesus Christ so that we are not moved by problems, obstacles, trials and tribulations.

- Sixth, the fellowship of His sufferings elicits God's help in getting our eyes off of ourselves and our own hurts and instead focus on the fellowship of His sufferings.

- Seventh, the fellowship of His sufferings means that Believers who live godly in Christ Jesus shall suffer persecution. We must realize the sufferings of this present age that we experience are not worthy to be compared with the glory which shall be revealed in us and we shall receive an eternal weight of glory for our momentary and light afflictions. Also, the God of all grace, who called us unto His eternal glory by Christ Jesus, after we have suffered a while, make us perfect, establishes, strengthens and settles us (Romans 8:18; 2 Corinthians 4:17; 1 Peter 5:10).

- Eighth, the fellowship of His sufferings prepares Believers to reign with Jesus Christ. God has predestined that Believers be made kings unto God. We shall also be priests of God and of Christ, reigning with Him a thousand years (the Millennial Kingdom) (Revelation 1:6; 3:21; 5:10; 20:4, 6).

That we may be also glorified together. Believers must have faith, hope and confidence in Jesus Christ that our vile bodies will eventually be transformed and fashioned like unto His glorious body and patterned after Jesus Christ's resurrection body (Philippians 3:20-21). We know from 1 Peter 5:10 that the Father has called us unto His eternal glory by Christ Jesus. Additionally, the glory and its eternal weight which shall be revealed in us refers to the future glory that is not yet fully revealed to us. Our future glory will occur when we appear with Jesus Christ as He appears to the world during His second coming and the rapture of the Church. At this time, Believers will appear and shall be like Him and shall see Him as He is.

"When Christ, who is our life, shall appear, then shall ye also appear with Him in glory" (Colossians 3:4).

"Beloved, now are we the sons of God and it doth not yet appear what we shall be: but we know that, when He shall appear, we shall be like Him; for we shall see Him as He is" *(1 John 3:2).*

When Jesus Christ fully reveals His glory at His second coming, the Believers who suffered and faithfully served Jesus Christ will forever be partakers of Jesus Christ's eternal glory.

"The elders which are among you I exhort, who am also an elder and a witness of the sufferings of Christ and also a partaker of the glory that shall be revealed" *(1 Peter 5:1).*

Chapter 22

I AM MORE THAN A CONQUEROR

"Yet in all these things we are more than conquerors through Him who loved us" (Romans 8:37).

T he word of God tell us in Romans 8:37 that our eternal Father fearfully and wonderfully made us to be more than a conqueror in Jesus Christ. This should not be a mere cliché or just religious words. We need to see ourselves as God sees us, because that's who we really are. We are more than conquerors! This means we are someone who has won more than an ordinary victory. A conqueror is someone who overpowers and achieves a decisive and abundant victory by crushing their enemies. More than a conqueror should become part of the identity and self-image of every Believer. Being more than a conqueror empowers and causes us to embrace and fulfill Reality Three – *By the Grace of God I Am What I Am!*

God did not intend for Believers to be defeated, anxious, confused, dismayed, distressed, nor under the dominion of darkness. We all face challenges and difficult situations, but in all these things we are to be overcomers and victorious in life as more than a conqueror and not just a survivor. But Satan, the defeated foe, holds some Believers in bondage. Our adversary is binding the very ones who should be dominating him. How is this possible? Why is this happening in the Body of Christ? Unfortunately, our defeated altitude keeps us from walking a victorious life as more than a conqueror. We are battle scarred but not victorious. We exercise some power but not authority. We survive but do not dominate that which we have defeated. Although we have overcome, we are not more than a conqueror.

As Believers we tend to concentrate on, testify and talk about the battles that we have won, but never win the war, nor dominate and take authority over the territory we have gained. Oftentimes, we hear people talk about their battle scars and say statements such as:

- *I made it through*
- *I am a cancer survivor*

- *I am holding on*
- *I am getting by*
- *I am just taking it one day at a time*
- *I am just barely making it*

By doing this, we are attempting to glorify God in our battle scars. We are quick to testify about our battle scars and what we overcame. But, God looks for and demands glory in victory *as more than a conqueror and not just a survivor!*

In order to be more than a conqueror and not just a survivor, it is essential for a Believer to embrace, understand and become a doer of six basic fundamental principles associated with being more than a conqueror. These basic fundamental principles are:

- *God's word*
- *Power*
- *Authority*
- *Dominion*
- *Submission*
- *Victory*

The Body of Christ must learn and position itself to confront Satan as more than a conqueror with these God-given fundamental principles. Satan and his fallen angels cannot endure that. The devil knows he is a defeated foe and tries to prevent the Body of Christ from realizing these spiritual truths that would cause us to be more than a conqueror.

God's Word

We must understand first of all that we are more than a conqueror, because the word of God says we are. God, through His word identified, purposed and predestinated us as more than a conqueror before the foundation of the world. The moment God said, *"Let us make man in our image, after our likeness"* His word went forth out of His mouth to accomplish that which God pleases – to give us an identity as more than a conqueror as well as the unique ability to embrace and fulfill Reality Three – *By the Grace of God I Am What I Am!*

God's word is our lifeline, shield and breastplate of victory (Romans 8:37). As more than a conqueror, we have the God-given right, **power, authority** and **dominion** to dominate and cause our enemy, problems, situations and circumstances to submit to us. Chief among our woes is Satan. It is time for the Body of Christ to realize that Satan, the adversary, is a *defeated foe* and rise up and take dominion over him.

Satan is a defeated foe because our Savior, Jesus Christ, defeated him, destroyed his works, spoiled his power and triumphed over him. Jesus Christ did all this for us, for the Body of Christ, so that His Church could be more than a conqueror and take authority and dominion over our adversary, our enemy and govern our sphere of influence.

> *"He that commits sin is of the devil; for the devil sins from the beginning. For this purpose the Son of God was manifested, that he might destroy the works of the devil" (1 John 3:8).*

> *"And having spoiled principalities and powers, he made a show of them openly, triumphing over them in it" (Colossians 2:15).*

Power and Authority

As more than a conqueror, we have to become familiar with power and authority. Everyone wants power and frequently talks about the power of God, but we rarely think about authority because the Body of Christ today often thinks that these two fundamental principles of being more than a conqueror are the same thing. But, they are not! Our Heavenly Father provided us with both power and authority and the Scriptures plainly distinguish between the two. A study of the life of Jesus Christ quickly reveals that our Savior displayed both power and authority (Luke 4:32, 36; 9:1). Subsequently, in order to exercise our God proclaimed right to be more than a conqueror, Believers must understand and distinguish the difference between power and authority.

- *Power – The ability to defeat and conquer your enemies, foes, and strongholds.*
- *Authority – The ability to rule over, govern and dominate your enemies, foes, and strongholds. The right and power to enforce obedience on a person or group to regulate or modify its behavior or censure improper behavior and to initiate correction (2 Corinthians 10:8).*

Notice that power only consists of the ability to defeat and conquer. On the other hand, authority goes beyond that, and comprises the ability to rule, govern, dominate, enforce, modify and correct.

Often we, through the Holy Spirit, exercise power or the ability to defeat and conquer obstacles, problems, situations, circumstances, hurdles and other distressing things in our lives. But, we fail to take the next step that is vital to becoming more than a conqueror – taking authority or the ability to rule, govern, dominate, enforce, modify and correct. The Body of Christ seldom takes authority over the very things it just defeated and conquered through its God-given birthright as a child of Almighty God.

Even though power and authority are not the same, both are important and necessary in our life. Jesus Christ, throughout His ministry, displayed both power and authority. This is evident when Jesus calmed a storm and healed the demon-possessed man. In both of these situations Jesus Christ displayed power over the wind and the demons.

Then He displayed His authority by saying unto the sea, *"peace, be still"* and commanding the demons to go. The wind, the sea and the demons all yielded to Jesus Christ's authority and obeyed His commands (Matthew 8:23-32; Mark 4:35-39; 5:1-14). It is important to note that obeying only comes because of authority. Additionally, Jesus Christ's authority caused the demons to shriek before the Lord Jesus Christ ever uttered a word.

The demons cried with a loud voice and said *"what have I to do with thee, Jesus, thou Son of the most high God? I adjure thee by God, that thou tor-ment me not."* It is interesting to note that the demons recognized Jesus Christ's authority before He did or said anything. Likewise, King Toi of Hamath recognized David's authority to rule, dominate, enforce, modify and correct even before David invaded his country. Recognizing David's authority, he brought David gifts of wealth (2 Sam 8:10). It is clear that power is seen only after we display it, but authority is recognized before we do anything.

Dominion

Now that we have an understanding of the first three basic fundamental principles (God's word, power and authority) let us look at dominion, the fourth basic fundamental principle associated with being more than a conqueror.

"And God said, Let us make man in our image, after our likeness: and let them have dominion over the fish of the sea, and over the fowl of the air, and over the cattle, and over all the earth, and over every creeping thing that creepeth upon the earth" (Genesis 1:26).

"And God blessed them, and God said to them, Be fruitful, and multiply, and replenish the earth, and subdue it: and have dominion over the fish of the sea, and over the fowl of the air,

and over every living thing that moveth upon the earth" (Genesis 1:28).

Genesis 1:26 states that God's purpose for man's relation to the creature is a relation of sovereignty. *Let us make man in our image, after our likeness* causes man to resemble God, qualifies man for dominion (the right and power to command, decide, rule, or judge) and constitutes man as the lord of all creatures.

Dominion is man's natural stewardship of the earth. Man's dominion extends from the fish of the sea to over all the earth to every creeping thing that creeps upon the earth and flies in it. As you can readily see, Genesis 1:26 lets us know that being more than a conqueror, we have the God-given right to dominate and cause our enemy, problems, situations, circumstances and everything that creeps upon the earth to submit to us. The Body of Christ is so mesmerized with bragging and testifying that it conquered something that it fails to realize the very thing it conquered can reassert itself if we do not dominate, take authority and cause it to submit to our authority.

Dominion is very important to being more than a conqueror. In Genesis 27:40 we see that it is our dominion, for instance, that breaks the yoke from off our neck that tries to ensnare us. Even though David's enemies possessed the land, David nevertheless asserted his power and authority. He then proceeded to take dominion over his enemies and recovered his border at the river Euphrates. Like David, we also have to take dominion and recover both everything the enemy took and tried to take away from us (2 Samuel 8:3; 1 Chronicles 18:3).

So if you are facing obstacles and hurdles that are weighing you down, take dominion over them. It is time for the Body of Christ to rise up and exercise its God-given right to dominate everything it conquers!

Submission

Submission is the fifth basic fundamental principle associated with being more than a conqueror. Submission involves yielding to the authority, power, or desires of another and allowing one's self to be subjected to them. David's military successes illustrates the principle of submission. David not only conquered his enemies but dominated, took authority over them and caused them to obey and submit to him. He even established a strong presence by putting garrisons in Syria and Edom, in the midst of his enemies, causing them to become his servants resulting in the subdued enemies bringing gifts to David (2 Sam 8:6-8,10,14). When we please God and take authority and dominion as more than a conqueror, God will make even our enemies to be at peace with us.

Another aspect of submission is it enables us to be more than a conqueror through Jesus Christ who strengthens us when we submit to God. Our submission to God and His holy ways provide us the strength necessary to resist the devil and cause him to flee in submission to our authority (James 4:7). Not only does our power, authority and dominion cause the devil to flee in submission, it also weakens his strongholds so we can recover everything the enemy took and tried to take away from us.

We know from the word of God that the devil is a thief. Therefore, the thief's submission not only weakens his stronghold, it forces him to restore sevenfold and give all the substance of his house to Believers who know they are more than a conqueror (Proverbs 6:31; Matthew 12:29; Luke 11:21-22). That is why it is time for the Body of Christ to stop bragging and testifying about how we conquered something and realize that the very thing we conquered can reassert itself if we do not take authority and dominion over it and cause it to submit to our authority. Once the Body of Christ does this it will readily discover how easy it is to embrace and fulfill Reality Three – *By the Grace of God I Am What I Am!*

Victory

Victory is the last basic fundamental principle associated with being more than a conqueror. The commandment of God teaches Believers that victory is the result of standing firm in the face of overwhelming odds, never wavering, but believing and trusting in the King of Glory. Victory means that despite the obstacles we face in life, we lean not unto our own understanding, but in all our ways acknowledge God and allow Him to direct our paths. Victory is achieved when we overcome and rise above all our problems, situations, circumstances and adversities in our life by faith in our Almighty Father.

"For whatsoever is born of God overcometh the world: and this is the victory that overcometh the world, even our faith. Who is he that overcometh the world, but he that believeth that Jesus is the Son of God?" (1 John 5:4-5)

Herein is a great biblical truth – our faith is the victory because through faith, Believers can stand fast and depend on the victory Christ has already won. Satan is a defeated foe because our Savior, Jesus Christ, defeated him, destroyed his works, spoiled his power, overcame and triumphed over him. All Believers should know in their hearts that in Jesus Christ we are more than conquerors because we have peace in Him and that Jesus Christ has already overcome the world (John 16:33). God has also given us power to overcome the world through Jesus Christ. He wants us to exercise power, take authority and dominion, especially since Jesus Christ has already overcome the world, or in other words, Jesus Christ deprived the world of the power to harm us and conquered the world for us. Because of Christ's victory, afflictions, problems, situations, obstacles, circumstances and adversities should not be able to easily beset and hold us in bondage nor have dominion over us.

A study of David's military successes as found in 2 Samuel Chapter 8 and 1 Chronicles Chapter 18 helps us to further understand what the word of God means by victory. In the face of overwhelming odds all about him, David's trust, faith, commitment and dependency in the Lord caused him to believe without a doubt and understand with great certainty that he would be victorious over his enemies. David not only conquered his enemies, but established a strong presence, dominated, took authority over them and caused them to submit and obey him. Likewise, the Body of Christ needs to accept victory in the midst of trials and tribulations by learning to rule and take authority over every single trial and tribulation that comes its way.

Just like David, we must understand and fully walk in the fact that in everything we face God through Jesus Christ gives us the victory. We need to get it in our hearts that the King of Glory, the Lord strong and mighty, mighty in battle, fights for us and gives us the victory. Not only did God inspire David's conquests and dominance, God preserved (guarded, protected and kept) David wherever he went. In other words, the Lord not only gave David victory, He also protected and kept him from his many enemies and adversaries.

God Protects. *"Yea, though I walk through the valley of the shadow of death, I will fear no evil: for thou art with me; thy rod and thy staff they comfort me" (Psalm 23:4).*

"...It is better to trust in the Lord...I will destroy them" (Psalm 118:9-12).

God Preserves. *"...And behold, I am with thee and will keep thee in all places whither thou goest..." (Genesis 28:15).*

"...be not afraid, neither dismayed; for the Lord thy God is with thee whithersoever thou goest..." (Joshua 1:5, 9).

Psalm 118:24 provides further understanding what the word of God means by victory. Unfortunately, *"This is the day which the Lord hath made; we will rejoice and be glad in it"* has become a cliché. Believers quote this scripture all the time without understanding and wisdom about what the scripture entails and unfortunately miss out on a wonderful blessing of victory. It is time to stop tossing Psalm 118:24 around like a tired worn out cliché and speak and confess it with understanding, wisdom, power and authority. When we understand two very essential aspects of Psalm 118:24 (David's military success and Jesus Christ as the chief cornerstone) and their relationship to victory we will not any longer speak Psalm 118:24 as a cliché but in wisdom, power and authority.

We already studied David's military success. Now let us see how Psalm 118:24 portrays his military victory as it relates to Psalm 118:5, 10-12. These verses wonderfully express David's confidence, trust and faith in God that He would give him victory over the many nations as well as his enemies. David was so confident that God would give the victory that three times he declared, *"I will destroy them."* Additionally, David walked in the knowledge and wisdom that it is the King of Glory who preserves and keeps us everywhere we go. When David thought back on that day, he remembered all of God's goodness, as well as God's great and merciful kindness toward him and that the truth of the Lord endured forever. This remembrance of the day that God had made caused David to praise and give thanks unto the Lord. Subsequently, David came to know Psalm 118:24 as being a day of victory, power, authority, dominion, salvation and preservation, which is why he was glad and rejoiced in the day that God had made.

The Body of Christ, like David, has reasons for our victory as more than a conqueror, such as:

- Our faith in God to give us victory over all afflictions, problems, situations, obstacles, circumstances and adversities
- Many are the afflictions of the righteous, but the Lord delivered him out of them all
- To know, without wavering, that we will destroy all our enemies because we trust in, lean on and depend on the Lord
- Embrace that the Lord is our strength and through Him we have the victory

- Reliance on the Lord as the King of Glory, strong and mighty and mighty in battle
- It is the Lord who fights our battles

We must also understand that prophetically Psalm 118:24 is a second advent passage that deals with thou art the Christ, the Holy One, the Son of God, the Lamb of God, Jesus Christ. The heart of Psalm 118 is verse 22.

"The stone which the builders refused is become the head stone of the corner (the chief cornerstone)."

In this verse we find one of the most important messianic prophesies dealing with the rejection and eventual restoration of Jesus Christ. Even though the Jewish nation commonly recited this messianic prediction at Passover, the builders of the religious system for the Nation of Israel rejected Jesus Christ as the stone. As a matter of fact, during Jesus' dispute with the religious leaders in Matthew 21:42, Jesus Christ quoted Psalm 118:22-23 to show the Pharisees how it related to His present rejection, and eventually His ultimate triumph as the head stone of the corner (the chief cornerstone) and foundation of the Church and our Christian faith.

What is this day that the Lord has made and why should we rejoice and be glad in it? Salvation is the reason why. Salvation is an important element of Psalm 118:24 in regards to the day that the Lord has made. Salvation is so important the word is mentioned three times in the Psalm.

"The Lord is my strength and song and is become my salvation" (Psalm 118:14).

"The voice of rejoicing and salvation is in the tabernacles of the righteous: the right hand of the Lord doeth valiantly" (Psalm 118:15).

"I will praise thee: for thou hast heard me and art become my salvation" (Psalm 118:21).

As we reflect on these three verses it becomes apparent that Psalm 118:24 is speaking of the day that God made for Jesus Christ to lay down His life as a sacrifice for our sins and become the chief cornerstone of the Church and our Christian faith. We witness the linkage between the stone (the chief cornerstone) and our salvation in Luke 20:18.

"Whosoever shall fall upon that stone shall be broken; but on whomsoever it shall fall, it will grind him to powder."

To fall upon this stone and be broken is a picture of our salvation from sin. We need God's salvation, for all have sinned and come short of the glory of God. On the flip side, *on whomsoever it shall fall*, refers to the judgment on those individuals who refuse to recognize and accept Jesus Christ as their Savior. The moment we fall upon the stone, broken and accept Jesus Christ as our Lord and Savior, we receive God's salvation, and the Holy Spirit comes to dwell within us. The Father and the Son also make their home within us in our hearts. That is why God made this day and we should rejoice and be glad in it, for it is the day of salvation and the day that Jesus Christ dwells within us.

So, the next time you hear someone say, *"This is the day which the Lord hath made; we will rejoice and be glad in it,"* realize that it is more than a tired worn out cliché and reflect on what this scripture really means. Why we should rejoice and be glad in it? Because this is a

- *Day of Victory* – *As more than a conqueror*
- *Day of Power* – *The ability to defeat and conquer your enemies, foes, and strongholds*

- <u>*Day of Authority*</u> – *The ability to rule over and dominate your enemies, foes, and strongholds. The right and power to enforce obedience on a person or group to regulate or modify its behavior or censure improper behavior and to initiate correction*

- <u>*Day of Dominion*</u> – *The right and power to command, decide, rule, or judge. Dominion over every bondage and to break every yoke*

- <u>*Day of Salvation*</u> – *The day that God made for Jesus Christ to lay down His life as a sacrifice for our sins and become the cornerstone, the chief cornerstone of the Church and our Christian faith*

- <u>*Day God Preserved You Everywhere*</u> – *And behold, I am with thee and will keep thee in all places whither thou goest*

- <u>*Day God is With You and Christ in You*</u> – *The Father and the Son also make their home within us in our hearts.*

Chapter 23

I AM THE HEAD AND NOT THE TAIL

*"And the LORD shall make you the head, and
not the tail; and you shall be above only, and
you shall not be beneath; if that you listen to
the commandments of the LORD your God,
which I command you this day, to observe and
to do them" (Deuteronomy 28:13).*

The Lord promises us blessings for our obedience.
That is why when we obey and observe God's
commandments, He promises to make us the head
and not the tail. It is worthwhile to momentarily
reflect on the symbolism and meaning of what the
"head" is. First, the symbolism of the word head, both
in Bible as well as ancient times was very important.
People culturally related anything that had power,
especially if it was derived from or associated with

authority, wisdom and control, to the head. Second, in Deuteronomy 28:13 the word refers to rulers, governors and leaders in any position. Just as in the Bible and ancient times, people today consider the head to refer to the person in charge who distributes decisions for the body to execute.

We must understand that it is God's leadership, in and through us, that makes others willing to follow. Our eternal Father promises that as the head, we should always be on the top and walk and live a victorious life as more than a conqueror. When God makes us the head, we will face challenges and difficult situations as overcomers and as more than a conqueror and not just a survivor rather than succumb to the challenges and situations as the tail – subservient, submissive and dominated by challenges.

By contrast, the head exercises power, authority and dominion over all challenges, obstacles and strongholds faced by the individual. The head habitually turns to, depends on and trusts in the Lord. The head knows without a shadow of doubt that God is able to make all grace abound toward it so that it will always have sufficiency in all things that may abound to every good work. In other words, God is able to make all grace (every favor and earthly blessing) come to the head in abundance so that the head may always and under all circumstances and whatever the need lacks nothing. The eternal Father makes it possible for the head to possess provisions exceedingly and abundantly above all that the head can ask or think according to the power that works in it. Subsequently, the head *shall always be above only and shall not be beneath!*

Deuteronomy 28:13 further teaches Believers that we should be above only and not beneath, if we listen to the commandants of the Lord. When we listen to the commandants of the Lord and stand firm in the face of overwhelming odds, never wavering but believing and trusting in the King of Glory, we will be above only and shall never be beneath. God wants us to be the head. God desires that we should be above. God moves on our behalf despite the obstacles we face in life when we lean not unto our own understanding but in all our ways acknowledge and allow Him to direct our paths. In essence, Deuteronomy 28:13 means that we are above all, victorious, more than a conqueror, overcomers, able to succeed in anything and receive blessings from God, if we pay attention to the commandants of the Lord and carefully follow them.

Our eternal Father fearfully and wonderfully made us the head and not the tail and gave us an identity laced with the ability to embrace and fulfill Reality

Three – *By the Grace of God I Am What I Am!* As we embrace and walk in Reality Three we soon discover we are the head. Further, we will understand that because our eternal Father fearfully and wonderfully made us the head, He will lift our heads up so we can stand tall, take power, authority and dominion over all our obstacles, problems, situations, circumstances, hurdles and other distressing things in our lives.

Chapter 24

I AM HIS PEOPLE AND HIS SHEEP

"For He is our God; and we are the people of His pasture, and the sheep of His hand. Today if ye will hear His voice" (Psalm 95:7).

"Know ye that the LORD He is God: it is He that hath made us, and not we ourselves; we are His people, and the sheep of His pasture" (Psalm 100:3).

"And ye shall be my people and I will be your God" (Jeremiah 30:22).

What does it mean to be His people and His sheep? Simply put, the Lord is our shepherd and we shall not want because we can trust and depend on the good shepherd, our Savior, Jesus Christ, to work everything together for the good of our welfare, and our God shall supply all our needs according to His riches in glory by Christ Jesus. Additionally, Jesus Christ, the good shepherd, sustains, comforts, leads us to safety, feeds and protects His people and His sheep. God and Jesus, the Christ, care for and seek an intimate and personal relationship with His people and His sheep.

That is why God is able to call each of them by name. As a matter of fact, God declares that He formed and redeemed us, called us by our name and engraved or wrote our names upon the palms of His hands (Isaiah 43:1; 49:16). God is so mindful of His people that He knows the number of hairs on each of our heads. This equates to the eternal security of God's salvation for His people and His sheep. God fearfully and wonderfully made us in His image and likeness as His people and His sheep so that we can embrace and fulfill Reality Three—*By the Grace of God I Am What I Am!*

Likewise, when we enter a close personal and intimate relationship with the good shepherd, we enjoy certain divine privileges. God declares by His holy word that He is predominantly, among other things:

- A hiding place, a secret place and a pavilion
- A rock

- A shield and a buckler
- A refuge and a source of strength
- A refuge and a fortress
- A deliverer
- An assurance for Believers

A Hiding Place, a Secret Place and a Pavilion

Those who earnestly seek the face of the Lord with their whole heart and being will not only find Him, but God will draw them into His hiding place, the secret place, the pavilion of the Almighty. It is in this secret place that we abide under the shadow of the Almighty. It is in this secret hiding place that God communes with us and carries us into the inner depths of His heart.

In the secret hiding place, the pavilion of God, He becomes everything. As far as we can see, there is nothing but God, Himself. In the secret hiding place, everything we touch and encounter is God and more of God. In the secret of His pavilion, God's will, desires and thoughts totally consume us. In the secret of His pavilion, we tap into God's mind and begin to spiritually see as the Father sees that all things are possible. Endless possibilities exist as far as we can see in all directions. In the secret of His hiding place,

our troubles and cares vanish only to be replaced by
the Spirit of the Lord, God's eternal being and all that
the Father is.

> *"For in the time of trouble He shall hide me in*
> *His pavilion: in the secret of His tabernacle*
> *shall He hide me; He shall set me up upon a*
> *rock" (Psalm 27:5).*

> *"Thou shalt hide them in the secret of thy*
> *presence from the pride of man: thou shalt*
> *keep them secretly in a pavilion from the strife*
> *of tongues" (Psalm 31:20).*

> *"Thou art my hiding place; thou shalt pre-*
> *serve me from trouble; thou shalt compass*
> *me about with songs of deliverance. Selah"*
> *(Psalm 32:7).*

> *"He that dwells in the secret place of the most*
> *High shall abide under the shadow of the*
> *Almighty" (Psalm 91:1).*

A Rock

In the beginning was the Word and the Word was
with God and the Word was God and His name is

called "The Word of God." The Word of God is none other than Jesus Christ, who is our spiritual Rock, a solid, firm foundation who is God eternal, the creator of all things (John 1:1; 1 Corinthians 10:4; Revelation 19:13). For the people of His pasture and the sheep of His hand, Jesus Christ is a Rock that we can trust, lean on and depend on.

Our LORD God lays in us a foundation, a stone, a tried stone, a precious corner stone, a sure foundation so that the people who believe will not act hastily, but, instead are secure in a sure foundation, remaining steadfast and immovable in the face of obstacles, problems, situations, circumstances, hurdles and other distressing things in their lives.

It is out of God's tender mercies and loving kindness that when our hearts are overwhelmed, He leads us to the Rock that is higher than us and a shelter and strong tower from the enemy. Furthermore, when we believe, trust, lean and depend on Jesus Christ as our rock we shall not be confounded or distressed. As Believers, we need to learn to trust in the LORD with all our heart and lean not unto our own understanding and in all our ways acknowledge Him.

When we do this, not only will He direct our paths but because we constantly keep the Almighty before our face, He will be on our right hand and uphold us with the right hand of His righteousness, so that we should not be moved. As God inclines and shows us His face, our spirit immediately knows beyond a shadow of a doubt that He only is our rock, our salvation, our fortress and our high tower.

We stare into the face of the Almighty, and without God uttering a single word our heart begins to declare "I shall not be greatly moved!" We will know with certainty that many are the afflictions of the righteous, but we shall not be greatly moved in times of afflictions because we can lean, depend and stand on the Rock with the expectation that God delivers His people out of all their afflictions.

We begin to understand that because Jesus Christ is the Rock, The Word of God, that without a shadow of doubt, He will lift our heads up so we can stand tall, take power, authority and dominion over all our obstacles, problems, situations, circumstances, hurdles and other distressing things in our lives.

"For in time of trouble He shall hide me in His pavilion: in the secret of His tabernacle shall He hide me; He shall set me up upon a rock. And now shall mine head be lifted up above mine enemies round about me: therefore will I offer in His tabernacle sacrifices of joy; I will

sing, yea, I will sing praises unto the LORD"
(Psalm 27:5-6).

"Bow down thine ear to me; deliver me
speedily: be thou my strong rock, for an house
of defense to save me. For thou art my rock
and my fortress; therefore for thy name's sake
lead me and guide me" (Psalm 31: 2-3).

A Shield and a Buckler

As a shield, God surrounds His people and His sheep with a divine hedge of protection. He protects and shields us on all sides, placing Himself between us, hurt, harm and evil. As our shield and buckler, God will not allow anything to touch us without it first touching Him. God Almighty will only allow those things to pass through the hedge of protection that He will use to mold and shape our heart and character. We can boldly proclaim, that as our shield and buckler God is our everything and we can lean on Him for all protection, knowing that He will never leave nor forsake us. Not only does God shield us, but He becomes our strength and stronghold.

"The LORD is my rock, and my fortress, and
my deliverer; my God, my strength, in whom

I will trust; my buckler, and the horn of my salvation, and my high tower" (Psalm 18:2).

"As for God, His way is perfect: the word of the Lord is tried: He is a buckler to all those that trust in Him" (Psalm 18:30).

"God is His people's strength and shield" (Psalm 28:7).

"Every word of God is pure: He is a shield unto them that put their trust in Him" (Proverbs 30:5).

A Refuge and a Source of Strength

For the people of His pasture and the sheep of His hand, God becomes a refuge and a source of strength. In God we can find a refuge from stress, worry and anxiety. He is a refuge for all those who are in trouble and brokenhearted. For us God is a place and a refuge to seek shelter. God is a source of strength to us in danger and a refuge we can flee to for safety. As our refuge and strength, through God we shall find rest unto our souls, and even though our flesh and our heart fails us, God is the strength of our heart and our portion forever.

203

In this place of refuge there is safety. The refuge is a place of protection. Peace and security abound in the refuge, just waiting for the people of His pasture to step into the Holy One's presence and partake of God's fellowship, goodness and tender mercies. It is in the refuge, the place of trust that we learn to put our trust in God at all times. In the refuge, we humble ourselves and begin to pour out our heart before God. God is a refuge for us so that we do not have to fear what man can do to us.

"The LORD also will be a refuge for the oppressed, a refuge in times of trouble" *(Psalm 9:9).*

"God is our refuge and strength, a very present help in trouble" *(Psalm 46:2)*

"I will say of the Lord, He is my refuge and my fortress: my God; in Him will I trust" *(Psalm 91:2).*

"I cried to you, O LORD: I said, You are my refuge and my portion in the land of the living" *(Psalm 142:5).*

*"The name of the LORD is a strong tower:
the righteous runneth into it and is safe"
(Proverbs 18:10).*

A Refuge and a Fortress

When we purpose a life of commitment, intimacy
and habitation with God, we come into God's care and
dwell in the secret place of the most High, and abide
under the shadow of the Almighty. In the secret place
of the most High, God is a fortress or a stronghold, a
safe place of shelter, providing defense and protection
that is impregnable. In essence, for the people of His
pasture and the sheep of His hand, Jesus Christ is a
place of refuge, a shelter, a fortress, protection and
cover from the storms of life that Believers encounter.

*"And he said, The LORD is my rock, and my
fortress, and my deliverer" (2 Samuel 21:2).*

*"Be thou my strong habitation, whereunto I
may continually resort: thou hast given commandment to save me; for thou art my rock
and my fortress" (Psalms 71:3).*

*"I am as a wonder unto many; but thou art my
strong refuge" (Psalms 71:7).*

"I will say of the LORD, He is my refuge and my fortress: my God; in Him will I trust" (Psalms 91:2).

"In the fear of the LORD is strong confidence: and His children shall have a place of refuge" (Proverbs 14:26).

A Deliverer

Believers can trust in the Lord that despite our many afflictions, He delivers us out of them all. Our Savior is saying to the Body of Christ, "For I the LORD thy God will hold thy right hand, saying unto thee, Fear not; I will help thee for I am a very present help in time of trouble. For it is the LORD who is our strength in the time of trouble." We must get this into our spirit that the Almighty says *"I will help thee."* Regardless of what we face or encounter, our Lord helps us overcome as more than a conqueror. We should not fear or let any situations, obstacles and problems dismay us, but realize in our spirit that we serve a loving Father and a Savior that is with us, and will keep us in all the places whither we go and never leave nor forsake us.

"Many are the afflictions of the righteous:
but the LORD delivereth him out of them all"
(Psalms 34:19).

"The Lord knoweth how to deliver the godly
out temptations and to reserve the unjust
unto the day of judgment to be punished" (2
Peter 2:9).

An Assurance for Believers

Jesus Christ gives Believers an assurance and securely guarantees that man will not pluck His people from His hands. Jesus Christ firmly upholds us with the right hand of His righteousness, saying unto us *"fear not for I am with thee: be not dismayed; for I am thy God."* Jesus Christ not only guarantees us safety in His hands, but in the Father's hands as well. The Prophet Isaiah put it this way, "Yea, before the day was I am He; and there is none that can deliver out of my hand: I will work and who shall let it?" Think about it, man cannot pluck Believers from Jesus Christ or the Father's hands.

This is a "double" guarantee and an assurance that in His hands it is impossible for us to suffer harm, damage or loss. Our heavenly Father gave us Jesus Christ, and He is greater than all of the united forces of humanity, the devil, fallen angels, demons and all enemies. It is a great comfort to know that tribulation, distress, persecution, peril, death, life, angels, principalities, powers, things present or to come, nor any other creature, shall separate us from the love of God, which is in Christ Jesus our Lord.

> *"And I give unto them eternal life; and they shall never perish, neither shall any man pluck them out of my hand. My Father, which gave them me, is greater than all; and no man is able to pluck them out of my Father's hand. I and my Father are one" (John 10:28-30).*

Furthermore, God so loved the world that He gave His only begotten Son for the salvation of the world. Jesus Christ, as the good shepherd was obedient unto death and gave His life for His people and His sheep that whosoever believeth in Him should not perish, but have everlasting life. The good shepherd came that His people and His sheep might have life and that they might have it more abundantly.

> *"I am the good shepherd: the good shepherd giveth his life for the sheep" (John 10:11).*

As part of His eternal plan and ultimate purpose in dealing with mankind as His people and His sheep, God chose us to be His eternal people. Our Father wants habitation with His people. Habitation occurs when God dwells and abides among His people and His people dwell with Him. He will walk and dwell among us as our God so that we will have eternal fellowship with Him and our Lord, Jesus Christ. This is fully realized when God establishes and personally moves to the New Earth after the Millennium. In the New Earth, God's eternal people will witness the visible presence of God the Father, God the Son and God the Holy Spirit.

"And what agreement hath the temple of God with idols? For ye are the temple of the living God; as God hath said, I will dwell in them and walk in them; and I will be their God and they shall be my people" (2 Corinthians 6:16).

"And I heard a great voice out of heaven saying, Behold, the tabernacle of God is with men and He will dwell with them and they shall be His people and God Himself shall be with them and be their God" (Revelation 21:3).

Chapter 25

I AM THE RIGHTEOUSNESS OF GOD IN HIM

"For He hath made Him to be sin for us, who knew no sin; that we might be made the righteousness of God in Him" (2 Corinthians 5:21).

We all are sinners and fall short of the glory of God. Due to one man's sin, Adam, sin entered into the world and subsequently, we all are shaped in iniquity and conceived in sin. Adam's sin sentenced all of humanity to condemnation and death. Our life begins without even the possibility of a sinless life, instead beginning with a sinful nature. Generally most people believe an unborn child has never committed any acts of sin, and it is hard to believe otherwise. But the scriptures clearly point out that all of us come into the world with a sinful nature.

This sinful nature is passed down from generation to generation, all the way from Adam to this present generation. We may think it is not right or fair that we are born into sin and have a sinful nature because of what one man did. However, the wonderful news is that because of what another man, Jesus Christ, did, we are able to receive God's abundant provision of grace and the gift of righteousness. Consequently, just as the result of one, trespass resulted in condemnation for all men, so also the result of one act of righteousness provides the means of justification that brings life for all men. Just as through the disobedience of Adam many were made sinners, so also through the obedience of Jesus Christ, many will be made righteous. How glorious it is to be made the righteousness of God and embrace and fulfill Reality Three – *By the Grace of God I Am What I Am!*

To clearly comprehend what "I am the righteousness of God" means, we must first understand what the righteousness of God is. The righteousness of God is His righteous dealing with our sins and sinners on the basis of our Lord Jesus Christ's death. Jesus Christ's death made it possible for the eternal Father to be merciful to our unrighteousness, sins and iniquities and remember them not any more (Hebrews 8:12). Our Lord Jesus Christ's death literally paid the price

211

for us to come into a right relationship with God. For all have sinned and fall short of the glory of God, and due to sin we cannot measure up to the requirements of a holy, righteous God.

The only way we can come into this right relationship with God is to have faith and believe in Jesus Christ. We cannot obtain this righteousness by obedience to any law or by our own merits. We cannot earn God's acceptance and approval. It is only obtainable by having faith in Jesus Christ, which is why God accounted Abraham for righteousness.

> *"For if Abraham was justified by works, he has something to boast about, but not before God. For what does the Scripture say? 'Abraham believed God and it was accounted to him for righteousness'" (Romans 4:2-3).*

When we believe and have faith in Jesus Christ, the eternal Father looks at our life as totally righteous, not because we are perfect, but because when we believed in the eternal Father's ability to forgive us of our sins, He freely gave us the gift of righteousness. It is our faith that causes us to submit to the righteousness of God. It is our faith that prompts our soul and spirit to come into a vital union with the eternal Father in Jesus Christ and inevitably conform ourselves to the will of God. It is our faith in Jesus Christ that activates righteousness and makes us the righteousness of God in Him. It is our faith that mandates righteousness and delivers us into the hands of God as the righteousness of God in Jesus Christ so we can embrace and fulfill Reality Three – *By the Grace of God I Am What I Am!*

When we receive Jesus Christ as our Lord and Savior in our lives, we become the righteousness of God in Him. At that moment, Jesus Christ sees us as a totally righteous person before God Almighty, forgiving us of our sins, shortcomings and failures.

Chapter 26

I AM A CHOSEN GENERATION, A ROYAL PRIESTHOOD, AN HOLY NATION, A PECULIAR PEOPLE

"But you are a chosen generation, a royal priesthood, an holy nation, a peculiar people; that you should show forth the praises of Him who has called you out of darkness into His marvelous light" (1 Peter 2:9).

"Who gave Himself for us, that He might redeem us from all iniquity and purify unto Himself a peculiar people, zealous of good works" (Titus 2:14).

A t the heart of these verses lies one of the most fundamental issues of human life and existence – the issue of our God-given identity. Our God-given identity finds its foundation in the fact that not only are Believers a chosen generation, a royal priesthood and a holy nation, but a peculiar people as well. Before the foundation of the world, the eternal Father chose us to be a peculiar people to show forth His praise and be zealous of good works.

"Peculiar" by the world's standards may carry the connotation of weird, strange, odd or uncommon, but as Believers we must realize that in the Kingdom of God the word carries an entirely different meaning. Peculiar in the Scriptures is translated from peripoiesis, which means *"God's own possession."* Subsequently, 1 Peter 2:9 and Titus 2:14 are telling the Body of Christ that God, the eternal Father, chose us as His very own possession!

God fearfully and wonderfully made and chose us in Him before the foundation of the world, making us a peculiar people, redeemed by Jesus Christ, purchased by the precious blood of Jesus Christ and owned by the Holy Father and the only Begotten Son, Jesus Christ. We are God's possession, called to be holy and without blame before Him in love.

When God chose us as a peculiar people, He shaped eternity and fashioned destiny to fulfill His divine decision. Then out of eternity, destiny calls time and causes time to place a demand on and birth forth purpose. We need to understand that all God's reasons for destiny and purpose lie inside of God and not outside of Him to be brought to bear upon Him. But, they lie inside of God – that is, they are what God is and God's reasons for destiny and purpose spring out of what God is. God's purpose begins in His presence.

When we draw close to God, He draws close to us, and when we know the eternal Father as He is and make his presence our habitation, we will know His purpose. In His purpose, God places us as His chosen peculiar people and begins to shape the character and mold the heart of His possession so that we, as a peculiar people, complete our purpose and destiny according to His holy will.

As a peculiar people we are not part of the world system, but fellow citizens with the saints and of the household of God. As a peculiar people, God has raised us up and made us sit together in heavenly places in Christ Jesus, for our conversation is in heaven from whence also we look for our Savior, the Lord Jesus Christ. Even though Believers live on the earth, our citizenship is in heaven, and we are governed by God's invisible power that works in us. As such, we must be mindful that we sit in the heavenly places and our conversation is in heaven. Take particular note that—*our conversation is in heaven!* If we get this concept in our spirit and our heart, when we speak we will use the same power of conversation that is occurring in the heavenly places.

Jesus Christ had us in mind as a peculiar people, God's own possession, when He lifted up His eyes to heaven to intercede for us and said:

"I have given them thy word; and the world hath hated them, because they are not of the world, even as I am not of the world. I pray not that thou shouldest take them out of the world, but that thou shouldest keep them from the evil. They are not of the world, even as I am not of the world. Sanctify them through thy truth: thy word is truth" (John 17:14-17).

It is evident from Jesus Christ's intercession that we are not of the world, but called to be a peculiar people, out of darkness and into His marvelous light that we may be blameless and harmless, the sons of God, without rebuke, in the midst of a crooked and perverse nation shining as lights in the world. In essence we, as God's own possession and a peculiar people, are the light of the world shining in God's brightness before the world to lead those in darkness to Jesus Christ. We are His possession, a peculiar people to embrace and fulfill Reality Three – *By the Grace of God I Am What I Am!*

Chapter 27

I AM CHOSEN OF GOD

"For many are called, but few are chosen"
(Matthew 22:14).

"According as He hath chosen us in Him
before the foundation of the world, that we
should be holy and without blame before Him
in love" (Ephesians 1:4).

"To whom coming, as unto a living stone,
disallowed indeed of men, but chosen of God
and precious" (1 Peter 2:4).

We are God's chosen, His elect. As such, God's pattern is to choose, call and shape us for an intimate and loving relationship with the King of Glory. When we open our heart, the eternal Father, the King of Glory, strong and mighty and mighty in battle comes in. As we draw close to God, He draws close to us to reveal more of Himself and as we begin to dwell in the secret place of the Most High, we shall abide under the shadow of the Almighty as His chosen and His elect. Further, we are chosen of God to offer up spiritual sacrifices such as presenting our bodies a living sacrifice, holy, acceptable unto God, which is our reasonable service.

Jesus Christ chose us out of the world. This is necessary to ensure we are not part of the world system. To be part of the world system is death, resulting in spiritual blindness to the eternal truth of God's word. If anyone loves the world the love of the Father is not in him.

Our eternal Father does not want us to be conformed to this world, its values and false belief systems, because the world is influenced by the prince of the power of the air and the demonic forces that shape it. It is a system of thoughts, motivation and ideas embedded in the flesh and very man-centered that ultimately does not seek after God for direction, leading and guidance.

Our eternal Father fearfully and wonderfully made, and chose us from the beginning for salvation as recorded in the following verses.

"But we are bound to give thanks always to God for you, brethren beloved of the Lord, because God hath from the beginning chosen you to salvation through sanctification of the Spirit and belief of the truth" (2 Thessalonians 2:13).

"Therefore I endure all things for the elect's sakes, that they may also obtain the salvation which is in Christ Jesus with eternal glory" (2 Timothy 2:10).

We need to understand that 2 Thessalonians 2:13 is telling us that God's choice for us is salvation through sanctification of the Spirit and belief of the truth. This is important because we can only receive salvation through these two things.

It is foolhardiness to claim salvation without sanctification and belief in the truth. Furthermore, our eternal Father chose and elected us before the foundation of the world to obtain salvation, which is in Christ Jesus with eternal glory. As a result of our Father choosing us, we not only obtain salvation but also the following blessings:

- Made holy by His Son, Jesus Christ's precious blood

- Set apart (separated) for the Lord, His holy work and service
- Accepted in the beloved of God
- Loved and cared for by the eternal Father

Chapter 28

I AM A ROYAL PRIEST

"And has made us kings and priests to God and His Father; to Him be glory and dominion forever and ever. Amen" (Revelation 1:6).

"And hast made us unto our God kings and priests: and we shall reign on the earth" (Revelation 5:10).

"Blessed and holy is he that hath part in the first resurrection: on such the second death hath not power, but they shall be priests of God and of Christ and shall reign with Him a thousand years" (Revelation 20:6).

God says to the Body of Christ that this day, we are in His image and likeness and created for Him so as royal priests we should show forth His praises in the earthen realm. God called us before the foundation of the world and we must rightly accept our spiritual identity as royal priests and establish this God-given royal priest identity in our hearts.

As royal priests we have the awesome and marvelous responsibility to minister unto the Lord, Jesus Christ. Minister finds its root in the Hebrew word "shareth," which accordingly means service and worshipper. Simply stated, to minister unto the Lord is indicative of our service and worship of the Lord, Jesus Christ. To "minister to the Lord" is to avail ourselves to serve Him by spreading the Gospel of Jesus Christ and to worship Him alone in all we do, to seek Him with our whole hearts and to seek first the kingdom of God and His righteousness.

Additionally, we have to exercise our spiritual authority by taking up the Cross of Prayer, intercession, and spreading the Gospel of Jesus Christ. We should saturate the atmosphere with God-focused prayer, intercession and worship. Furthermore, we must realize our great High Priest, Jesus Christ, hears the cries, sees the afflictions and knows the sorrows of people that He looks for, and calls forth an intercessor to intercede on behalf of them. As royal priests, we have unrestricted access to the King of Glory and can come boldly before the throne of grace and the

Almighty to obtain mercy, find grace to help in time of need and offer prayers for ourselves and others. Unlike the Levitical priesthood in Israel which was based on physical birth, the royal priesthood of the Believer is rooted in the principle that we are a new creature and a new man because of our entering into the new life covenant relationship with Christ Jesus as our Lord and Savior.

Oftentimes, Believers are amazed that our Father has appointed every Believer to be a royal priest, not just those who come from a special order or group among the Body of Christ. Our Father made all of us kings and priests unto Himself. Not only has God called us to be royal priests in the earthen realm, we will continue to hold our office as royal priests and reign with our King, Jesus Christ, for a thousand years during the Millennium.

Everything we experience in our lives, our sufferings, tribulations, trials and afflictions, are designed to prepare us to reign alongside the King of Glory. Therefore, we should find some solace in this spiritual truth and boldly walk in the knowledge that God works together for good to them that love God, to them who are the called according to His purpose, and our sufferings during this present time are not worthy to be compared with the glory which shall be revealed in us. Our destiny as royal priests of God and of Christ is what the eternal Father has in mind. This is why it behooves us to embrace and fulfill Reality Three – *By the Grace of God I Am What I Am!*

Chapter 29

I AM A NEW CREATURE AND A NEW MAN

"Therefore if any man be in Christ, he is a new creature: old things are passed away; behold, all things are become new" (2 Corinthians 5:17).

"And that you put on the new man, which after God is created in righteousness and true holiness" (Ephesians 4:24).

"For in Christ Jesus neither circumcision availeth anything, nor uncircumcision, but a new creature" (Galatians 6:15).

"And have put on the new man, which is renewed in the knowledge after the image of Him that created him" (Colossians 3:10).

We are a new creature and a new man because we have entered into the new life covenant relationship with Christ Jesus as our Lord and Savior. As part of this covenant relationship, the Lord gives us a new life and makes us a new creature and a new man in Himself. It is especially noteworthy to understand that this relationship is not dependent on what we do or do not do.

Jesus Christ, our Lord and Savior, established and initiated the relationship because of God's unconditional love. However, what we do or do not do affects our level of intimacy and fellowship with Jesus Christ. For instance, Adam's sin caused him to step out of intimacy and fall out of fellowship with God. However, the relationship between the eternal Father and Adam remained intact. When we draw close to God and diligently seek the Lord with all our heart, spirit, soul, strength and mind, He draws close to us, producing a deep level of intimacy and fellowship that our Lord and Savior desires.

Old things are passed away; behold all things are become new. In the new life covenant relationship the old things that are passed away consist of the old man's spirit, sinful nature and power of sin that dominated the old man. Let's take a moment to reflect on that old man's sinful nature that has passed away due to the new life covenant. The moment Adam stepped out of intimacy and fell out of fellowship with God, he introduced all of humanity to its sinful nature. Even though God said *"Let us make man in our image, after our likeness,"* following Adam's transgression, sin entered into the world and subsequently, we all are shaped in iniquity and conceived with a sinful nature.

Old things are passed away; behold all things are become new. This sinful nature alienates God from humanity because the sinful nature is contrary to God's nature. In other words, the sinful nature makes man (humanity) unlike our God in regards to His moral nature and character. God is in perfect holiness, while man's sinful nature consists of perfect iniquity and the two can never meet. That is why our old man is crucified with Jesus Christ so the body of sin might be destroyed and henceforth we should not serve sin. This is an important part of the new life covenant relationship, because the old man connects us to the world and the spirit, nature and power of the devil which is working in men to disobedience. It is the old nature that keeps us in darkness, causes us to think our way is right in our own eyes and blinds us from the truth of God's word.

Old things are passed away; behold all things are become new. When we enter into the new life covenant relationship we put off the old man, which is corrupt according to the deceitful lusts and renewed in the spirit of our mind. Being renewed in the spirit of our mind is the bridge between putting off the old man and putting on the new man. Also, when we are renewed in the spirit of our mind, it is renewed according to God's Spirit, nature and power. This enables us to partake of God's divine nature and escape the corruption that is in the world through lust. This is an important concept because our eternal Father does not want us to be conformed to this world, its values and false belief systems, but instead wants us transformed by the renewing of our mind by His word, His truth and His living Spirit, that we may prove what is that good, acceptable and perfect will of God.

Old things are passed away; behold all things are become new. When we put on the new man, we are renewed in knowledge after the image and spiritual likeness of the eternal Father who created us. Tragically, as a result of the fall of man, our heart is not any longer as God originally intended it to be. However, God intends to make a new heart within us, so it is with this part of ourselves that we believe in Him. It is also where the Spirit of God comes to dwell, pouring out divine love within us. Basically, at this moment in eternity when we put on the new man and are renewed in the knowledge of the Father, God takes our spirit back to its original state the way it existed before Adam's sin. When Adam fell, he stepped out of intimacy and fell out of fellowship with God. In its original state, our spirit freely communes with the eternal Father without obstructions or inhibitions. In our spirit's original state, we are able to know God's continual presence and the Heart of the Father and ours are one in unity, love, intimacy and fellowship.

Old things are passed away; behold all things are become new because Jesus Christ forgives us for our old nature, redeems us from a sinful past and makes all things new. Jesus Christ not only redeems us from our sinful past, He also forgives all our iniquities, blots out our sins and not any longer remembers our sins and iniquities. Jesus Christ gives us a new life and makes us a new creature so that we not any longer have to walk according to the course of this world, according to the prince of the power of the air, but as children of God and a new man, created according to God in true righteousness and holiness.

Old things are passed away; behold all things are become new that we should walk in newness of life, not after the flesh, but after the Spirit; in a newness of life that pleases God, the Father because we are not any longer in the flesh. A newness of life that identifies us with Jesus Christ, our Savior. A newness of life that lets the word of Christ dwell in the new man richly in all wisdom, teaching and singing with grace in our hearts to the Lord. A newness of life that allows the peace of God to rule in the new man's heart. A newness in life as a new man whose most fundamental characteristic is to put on love, which is the bond of perfection.

Old things are passed away; behold all things are become new. Ultimately, in this new life covenant relationship, the Lord gives us a new life and makes us a new creature and a new man in Himself so that we can enter into the kingdom of God and are not any longer carnally, but spiritually minded. This is important and essential to God because a carnal mind is death and enmity (hostile) against God. Further, a carnal mind is after and minds the things of the flesh. In other words, those who set their attention and affection on the sins of the flesh will ultimately satisfy those sinful desires. Whereas, to be spiritually minded is life and peace, which causes us to be in the Spirit so that the Spirit of God dwells in us. Now if any person has not the Spirit of Christ, that person cannot identify with Jesus Christ. But, as a new creature and a new man, the Spirit of the living God dwells in us and we are led by the Spirit of God and the Spirit itself bears witness with our spirit that we, as a new creature and a new man, are the sons and children of God.

Chapter 30

I AM HIS WORKMANSHIP

"For we are His workmanship, created in Christ Jesus unto good works, which God hath before ordained that we should walk in them" (Ephesians 2:10).

"If a man therefore purge himself from these, he shall be a vessel unto honour, sanctified and meet for the master's use and prepared unto every good work" (2 Timothy 2:21).

"Make you perfect in every good work to do His will, working in you that which is well pleasing in His sight, through Jesus Christ; to whom be glory forever and ever. Amen" (Hebrews 13:21).

First and foremost, we must understand that we are God's workmanship that He is preparing for Himself in order to show Himself to the world. Secondly, God will meticulously take His time to ensure His workmanship is made perfect in every good work to do His will, and He will work in us that which is well pleasing in His sight. Thirdly, even when our lives seem hectic, messy and out of control, we can rest assured and be confident of this very thing, that He which hath begun a good work in us will perform it until the day of Jesus Christ.

It is necessary for God to work in us that which is well pleasing in His sight. When He invites us to join in His purposes and works, He is already at work, shaping and molding our character. The Prophet Isaiah knew this all too well, which is evident by these words he spoke to the eternal Father, which should resonate in our heart and spirit. *"But now, O LORD, thou art our Father, we are the clay and thou our potter and we all are the work of thy hand."*

The reality of these words in Isaiah 64:8 reveal that we are clay in our eternal Father's hand and are not capable of shaping and molding our own character any more than a lump of clay is able to shape and mold itself. But the eternal Father is a skilled potter and in His hands He shapes and molds our marred character until it begins to take on the intended shape He intends for it to be. The character God shapes is indicative of one He has called out for His holy purpose. Further, this character is foundational to what God builds upon.

When our character and heart are not right and not in unity with the eternal Father's character and heart, we tend to approach the Lord with an empty basket syndrome rather than an open heart. The empty basket syndrome means we come to the Lord with our hands held out, telling the Lord what we need, begging Him to immediately move on our behalf. We then inform Him what we want, then impatiently wait for Him to fill our empty basket.

The empty basket syndrome is "me" centered and focused. On the other hand, a heart that is in unity with God's heart will approach the Lord not by seeking what is in His hands, but instead desiring to see His face. The open heart says, *"God, I just want more of You."* The open heart, unlike the empty basket heart, is God centered. Because of this focus, the eternal Father takes His time to shape, mold and develop our heart and character, because its state and character are essential to performing and accomplishing God's works. Subsequently, at the time of the invitation, God begins to shape and mold our hearts and character so we can complete His purposes and works as the servants of Christ, doing the will of God from our heart.

God has to shape, mold and develop our hearts and characters so that our lives flow into the center of His will in unity with His heart and character. The Heart of God and our heart must be unified! God wants to bring us from a place of just merely knowing Him to a place of profound, intimate communion, where His heart and our heart begin to commune in the most Holy Place. It is here that the unity of the Heart of God and our heart cause the work of our flesh to cease and the Heart of God to begin.

This union of hearts makes it possible for God to reveal, and for us to receive what is on the Heart of God. This divine union transcends beyond just hearing the voice of God and makes it possible for us to see what the Almighty is doing as well as what He plans to do. When our hearts are in unity and right with the Heart of God, we begin to bear all things, believe all things, hope all things, endure all things, trust all things and obediently do all things the eternal Father desires.

That is why it pleases Him when our heart diligently seeks after Him. God wants us to draw close to Him, not with our flattering mouth or by honoring Him with our lips, but with a heart that is close to Him and seeks after His very own Heart. God needs a heart and character that are totally God-purposed and driven, God-obedient, God-centered and God-focused.

God uses both positive and negative moments in our lives to shape, mold and develop our hearts and characters. We have to realize that nothing can touch us without first touching God. Further, God only allows those things to pass through that He will use to shape, mold and develop our hearts and characters to match His will. The eternal Father works these positive and negative moments together for good to those who love God, to those who are called according to His purpose. In the midst of our most negative moments in life, we must come to the realization that the word of God tells us to glory in tribulations, knowing that tribulation produces perseverance and perseverance, character and character, hope.

Our character is very important to the eternal Father. Not only that, but God's purpose is much greater than our problems, obstacles, pain, trials, tribulations and even our sin. When our hearts and characters remain true to God with trust, faith and confidence in Him, and align with His purposes, the LORD God proceeds to reveal more of His heart, His character, His purpose and His being to us.

As God's workmanship, not only does He shape, mold and develop our heart and character, He is also with us and keeps us in all the places we go, being very mindful of us and crowning us with glory and honor, setting us over His works. In essence, God fearfully and wonderfully made us, His workmanship is to have a character that matches His purposes, to have dominion over the works of His hands and put all things under our feet. This means that God predestined us to have power, authority and dominion over what He created – the works of His Hands (Psalm 8:4-9).

Chapter 31

I AM THE APPLE OF HIS EYE

*"Keep me as the apple of the eye, hide me under
the shadow of thy wings from the wicked that
oppress me, from my deadly enemies, who
compass me about" (Psalm 17:8-9).*

As we draw close to God, He draws close to us to reveal more of Himself, His Spirit, His nature and His being. The closer we draw to God, He is inclined to show us His face and our spirit immediately knows beyond a shadow of doubt that He only is our rock, our salvation, our fortress and our high tower.

During this divine encounter with God, we are staring into the face of the Almighty, and without God uttering a single word our heart begins to declare, "I shall not be greatly moved!" As we continue to stare, we see in the light of the King's face not just life, but abundant life. At this moment in eternity, God looks into our eyes lovingly staring at Him and sees His own image reflected in miniature. He also sees the mind of Jesus Christ and Jesus Christ's character and attitude being reflected in greatness and brightness before Him, leading souls to the Kingdom of God.

As the apple of His eye, God is not only very mindful of us, but draws us under the shadow of His wings where He cares for, defends and protects us from our deadly enemies and the wicked ones that try to oppress us. Basically, God does not let our enemies or the wicked touch the apple of His eye. This is what Psalm 17:8 means when it says *"Keep me as the apple of the eye."*

Chapter 32

I AM A TRUE WORSHIPPER

"But the hour cometh and now is, when the true worshippers shall worship the Father in spirit and in truth: for the Father seeketh such to worship Him. God is a Spirit: and they that worship Him must worship Him in spirit and in truth" (John 4:23-24).

John 4:23-24 tells us that a true worshipper worships God in spirit and in truth. But, what does it really means to worship God as a true worshipper? First, we must understand there is a fundamental difference between praise and worship.

The word of God tells us *"Let everything that has breath praise the LORD. Praise ye the Lord"* and to enter His courts with praise. Jesus Christ even said that if people do not praise the eternal Father, the *"stones will cry out."* Praise, simply put, is offering thanksgivings to the eternal Father, joyfully recounting all He has done for us and showing appreciation for His mighty works on our behalf. In essence, praise exclusively focuses on what God has in His hands, what He has to offer and what the eternal Father has done for us.

While praise can be a part of worship, worship goes beyond praise. Whenever the scriptures mention worship, the tone of the scriptures takes on the connotation that worship is a fear or a reverence of the Lord where desiring to seek His face outweighs the desire for what is in His Hands. Worship is God-focused and God-centered.

Worshiping God in spirit means we worship Him from the heart and "love the Lord thy God with all thy heart and with all thy soul, and with all thy mind and with all thy strength." Worship draws and causes you to abide in the secret place of the Almighty. Worship causes you to push past God's hands and brings you to a place where your heart is so enumerated with God, the eternal Father and Jesus Christ our Lord and Savior, that you do not care whether the eternal Father does anything for you at all.

Worship says whether He blesses me or not, I will still bow down, reverence and worship Him. Worship further arouses your heart to surrender to God's heart and motivates your spirit to fall down before He who sits on the throne and worship Him who lives forever and ever, while setting off shouts in your spirit of *"You are worthy, our Lord and God, to receive glory and honor and power."* Worship inspires your heart and provokes your spirit so that all you want and your only desire is to see God's face, to kneel and bow before His Holy being just because He is the Lord!

A true worshipper honors the eternal Father with a way of life that is pleasing to our Father and God. Worship becomes a lifestyle, not just an occasional activity. God, to a true worshipper, is the center of everything, the object of worship, the subject of worship and the focus of it all! Everything a true worshipper's spirit does in truth attests to this. A true worshipper worships God by simply believing the truth of God's holy word. Regardless of what God's holy word says, a true worshipper embraces and holds the truth of the word in his heart and does what the word says.

He wants all those who come near Him to glorify and worship Him in spirit and in truth. Worship in spirit and in truth is a deliberate, steady focused time with the Father, not on our terms, but on the Father's terms. True Worship involves loosing ourselves in the adoration of the eternal Father. It is through true worship that we invite the Holy Spirit to speak to us, convict us and comfort us. Through worship, we realign our priorities with God's, and acknowledge Him once more as the rightful Lord of our lives. It is through true worship that we can embrace and fulfill Reality Three – *By the Grace of God I Am What I Am!*

EPILOGUE

I AM FEARFULLY AND WONDERFULLY MADE

In the beginning God created the heaven and the earth. And God said, Let us make man in our image after our likeness and let them have dominion over the fish of the sea and over the fowl of the air and over the cattle and over all the earth and over every creeping thing that creepeth upon the earth.

God gave us an identity when He made us in His image and likeness in order to have dominion. Furthermore, our God and Father fearfully and wonderfully made us in His image and likeness so that we can fulfill three realities—*to God be the glory, I can do what the word says I can do and by the grace of God I am what I am*. He also gives us an identity uniquely tailored to and woven into His sacred and holy word. God's word ultimately leads one to conclude and believe God's three realities for humanity. We must understand that it is in these three realities that we will find our God-given identify. Our flesh is probably the greatest challenge our identity has to face and overcome, especially if we are not used to living our lives according to God's holy word and God's three realities for humanity.

EMBRACING THE THREE REALITIES

Believers who embrace these three realities soon begin to walk in the word, display the power of the word and exercise the authority of the word. Once we embrace these three realities it will cause us to realize our God-given identity and boldly walk in the fullness and reality of purpose and destiny that God predestined for each one of us before the foundation of the world. The Believers will understand their identity in the Father propels, motivates and drives them to glorify our Father and Creator, because in Him we live and move and have our being (Acts 17:28). Furthermore, Believers will come to realize that we can do what the word says we can do, and by the grace of God we are what we are because God, our Father, fearfully and wonderfully made us so. As a body of Believers we can only realize our true identity in God when we embrace and walk in the three realities.

THE GRACE OF LORD JESUS CHRIST
BE WITH YOU

May the grace of our Lord Jesus Christ be with you all as you realize your God-given identity and you begin to embrace and walk in the three realities—*to God be the glory, I can do what the word says I can do and by the grace of God I am what I am.* Amen.

BOOKS AND ARTICILES RESEARCHED AND STUDIED

Barker, Kenneth L. *New International Version, Study Bible*. Grand Rapids: Zondervan, 2008

Blackaby, Thomas. *Created to be God's Friend Workbook, Lessons from the Life of Abraham*. Nashville: Thomas Nelson Publishers, 2000

Bynum, Juanita. *The Threshing Floor*. Lake Mary: Charisma House a Strang Company, 2005

Dake, Finis, Jennings. *Dake's Annotated Reference Bible*. Lawrenceville: Dake Publishing, Inc., 1999

Hayford, Jack. *Spirit Filled Life Bible for* Students, New King James Version. Nashville: Thomas Nelson Publishers, 1982

Houdmann, Michael. "What Does 1 Peter 2:9 Mean When It Referes to Believers As Peculiar People?"

Gotquestions.org. http://www.gotquestions.org/ peculiar-people.html#ixzz2RLQILTcL (accessed December 10, 2013).

Houdmann, Michael. "What Is the Difference Between Praise And Worship?" Gotquestions.org. http://www/gotquestions.org/difference-praise-wor-ship.html#ixzz2WKvPRt31 (accessed December 10, 2013).

In Touch. "An Open Door to God's Glory." Intouch. org. http://www.intouch.org/magazine/content/topic/ An_Open_Door_to_God_s_Glory#.UuPjdiAo7mQ. (Accessed January 25, 2014)

James, Bruce. "And My Father Is The Husbandman." Truth Magazine XXIII: 38, September 27, 1979

LaHaye, Tim. *Prophecy Study Bible, King James Version.* AMG Publishers, 2000

Partow, Donna. *Becoming a Vessel of God's Power.* Colorado Springs: Waterbrook Press, 2007

Price, Paula. *The Prophet's Dictionary.* Tulsa: Flaming Vision Publications, 1992, 2002

Stanley, Charles F. "Promises to Heal." *In Touch,* August 2013

Stanley, Charles F. "When Facing Life's Mountains." *In Touch*, November 2013

Strong, James. *The New Strong's Complete Dictionary of Bible Words*. Nashville: Publishers, 1996

The Amplified Bible, Expanded Edition. Grand Rapids: The Zondervan Corporation and the Lockman Foundation, 1987

Tozer, A.W. *The Attributes of God, A Journey Into the Father's Heart, "I Am That I Am*. Camp Hill: The Christian Publication, 1997

Turner, Ray. "And I Said "Get Thee Behind Me Satan–But He Didn't." EzineArticles.com. http://EzineArticles.com/?expert=Ray Turner. (Accessed February 16, 2013)

Vine, W.E., Unger, Merrill, White, William. *Vine's Complete Expository Dictionary of Old and New Testament Words*. Nashville: Thomas Nelson Publishers, 1996

Warren, Rick. *The Purpose Driven Life*. Grand Rapids: Zondervan, 2002

Wilson, Walter L. *A Dictionary of Bible Types*. Peabody: Hendrickson Publishers, 1999

Word Press. "When in Need, Where do I Go? – Within the Holy Spirit." Wordpress.com. http://withintheholyspirit.wordpress.com/?s=When+in+Need%2C+Where+do+I+Go%3F+%E2%80%93+Within+the+Holy+Spirit. (Accessed December 10, 2013)

CPSIA information can be obtained at www.ICGtesting.com
Printed in the USA
BVOW07s1220230714

360168BV00001B/1/P